9/92

WINGS AROUND THE WORLD

9/92

Other Books by K. C. Tessendorf

KILL THE TSAR!
UNCLE SAM IN NICARAGUA
BARNSTORMERS & DAREDEVILS
ALONG THE ROAD TO SOWETO

WINGS AROUND

Wings

AROUND THE WORLD

The American World Flight of 1924

by **K. C. TESSENDORF**

ATHENEUM 1991 NEW YORK

COLLIER MACMILLAN CANADA   *TORONTO*

MAXWELL MACMILLAN INTERNATIONAL PUBLISHING GROUP
NEW YORK   OXFORD   SINGAPORE   SYDNEY

Acknowledgments and credits are to be found on page 104.

Atheneum
Macmillan Publishing Company
866 Third Avenue
New York, NY 10022

Collier Macmillan Canada, Inc.
1200 Eglinton Avenue East
Suite 200
Don Mills, Ontario M3C 3N1

Designed by Barbara DuPree Knowles

Map illustration by Virginia Norey

FIRST EDITION

LIBRARY OF CONGRESS CATALOGING-IN-PUBLICATION DATA
Tessendorf, K. C.
   Wings around the world: the American world flight of 1924 / by K. C. Tessendorf.—1st ed.
      p.   cm.
   SUMMARY: Describes the exploits of the first pilots to fly around the world.
   ISBN 0-689-31550-3
   1. Flights around the world—Juvenile literature. [1. Flights around the world. 2. Voyages around the world. 3. Aeronautics—Flights.] I. Title.
G445.T47 1991
910.4'1—dc20
90-977

Printed in the United States of America   1 2 3 4 5 6 7 8 9 10

Contents

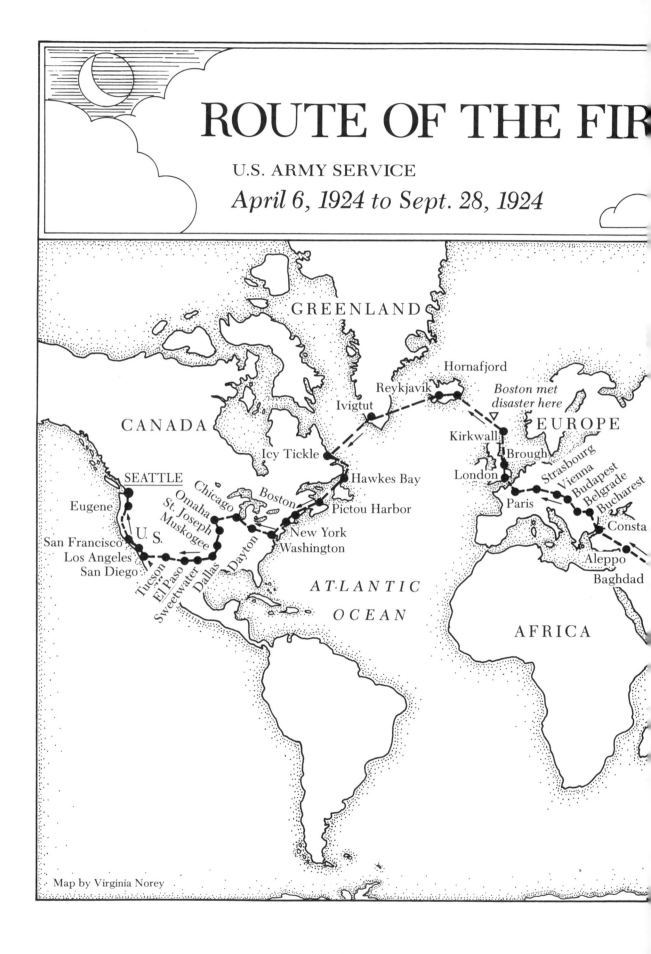

ROUTE OF THE FIR

U.S. ARMY SERVICE

April 6, 1924 to Sept. 28, 1924

GREENLAND

Hornafjord

Reykjavik

Boston met disaster here

Ivigtut

EUROPE

CANADA

Kirkwall

Icy Tickle

Brough

SEATTLE

Chicago

Boston

Hawkes Bay

London

Strasbourg

Vienna

Budapest

Eugene

Omaha

St. Joseph

Muskogee

Pictou Harbor

Paris

Belgrade

Bucharest

U. S.

New York

Washington

Consta

San Francisco

Los Angeles

San Diego

Tucson

El Paso

Sweetwater

Dallas

Dayton

ATLANTIC OCEAN

Aleppo

Baghdad

AFRICA

Map by Virginia Norey

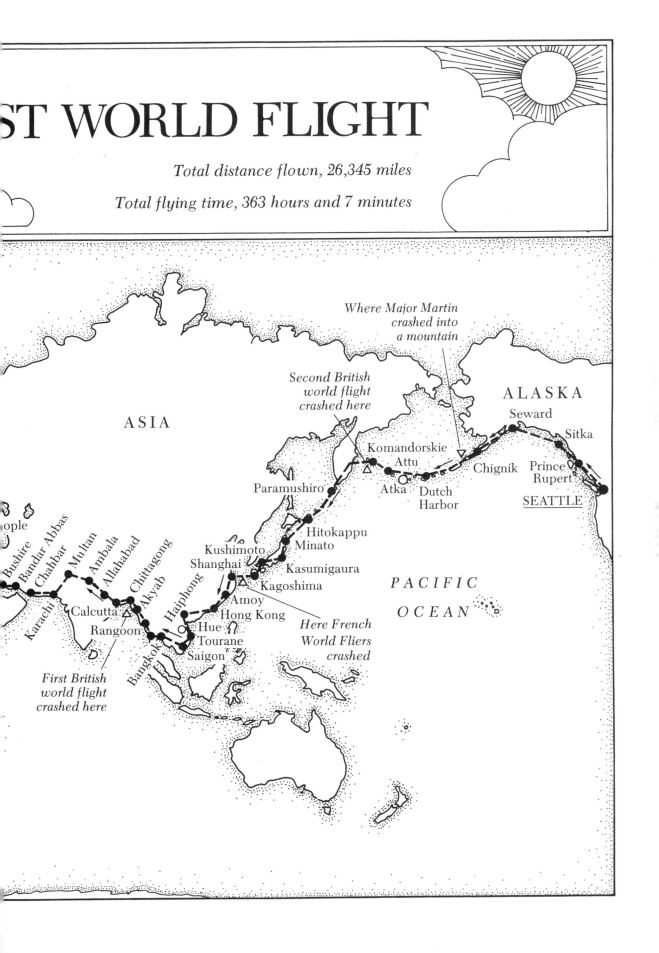

ST WORLD FLIGHT

Total distance flown, 26,345 miles

Total flying time, 363 hours and 7 minutes

Where Major Martin crashed into a mountain

Second British world flight crashed here

ALASKA

Seward

Sitka

ASIA

Komandorskie

Attu

Chignik

Prince
Rupert

Atka

Dutch
Harbor

SEATTLE

Paramushiro

ople

Bushire

Bandar Abbas

Chahbar

Multan

Ambala

Allahabad

Chittagong

Akyab

Hitokappu

Minato

Kushimoto

Shanghai

Kasumigaura

PACIFIC

Karachi

Calcutta

Rangoon

Haiphong

Kagoshima

Amoy

Hong Kong

Hue

Tourane

Saigon

Bangkok

OCEAN

*Here French
World Fliers
crashed*

*First British
world flight
crashed here*

For the intrepid and innovative airmen
of all the U.S. Armed Services
who endured lagging pay and promotion
to stay on the job between the wars
and be at hand when the nation
desperately needed them after 1941

Of what these world fliers did, we may well be proud, and I commend their story to our people who have always admired those who are willing to venture into new fields, to show themselves to be men undaunted by dangers, resourceful and unafraid.

—MAJOR GENERAL MASON PATRICK,
from *The First World Flight* by Lowell Thomas

CHAPTER ONE

The First Verse

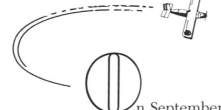

On September 28, 1924, two big Douglas World Cruisers—rugged, long-range, open-cockpit biplanes—landed at Seattle, Washington, on the 172nd day after their departure from there. Still piloted by their original air crews, the two World Cruisers had flown 26,345 miles over two oceans and three continents to complete the first around-the-world flight. It was one of the greatest accomplishments in the "stick, wire and canvas" era of aviation history. In saluting their feat, an aviation magazine quoted English author Rudyard Kipling: "We are at the first verse of the opening page of the chapter of endless possibilities."

This book tells the high adventure of flying around the world in 1924. Daily, these intrepid American airmen risked their necks, often flying where no aircraft had been before. They had to cope with the emergencies caused by extremes of arctic cold and tropic heat on the fabric-covered airplanes with barely adequate engines, guided by primitive instruments. They surely did write Kipling's "first verse" for world-class aviation, and they were hailed as "Magellans of the air" after the sixteenth-century sea captain whose ships first sailed around the world.

Though daily risking their lives, they were, with a major exception, well-fed and -housed on every evening of their journey. Indeed,

The four Douglas World Cruisers of the first around the world flight in a painting by Robert Sherry

the celebrations for them in the twenty-two foreign nations they visited became an "ordeal by banquet." On the other hand, not every flier made it all the way around. Four Douglas World Cruisers flew out of Seattle, but only two returned.

The military needs of World War I speeded up the development of aircraft technology. When the war was over, a vast surplus of aircraft and trained pilots remained. A few of these pilots dared to believe that they could fly around the world, and in 1922, Norman MacMillan, a superb Royal Air Force pilot in the war, obtained English financial backing for his proposed around-the-world flight. He planned to use four different aircraft, each chosen for a specific segment of the trip.

Flying a former RAF plane in a thrill-a-flight journey, MacMillan reached Calcutta, India, a quarter of the way around the world from London. His second aircraft, a pontooned seaplane, had arrived by ship from England. But the strong tropic sun and hot air had caused a crack in one pontoon, as MacMillan discovered soon after floating the plane. There was no effective sealant available in India, nor was there the expertise to build a new pontoon. To wait for a replacement pontoon from Britain would upset his schedule for crossing the far north Pacific in good weather. It might have been wisest for him to cancel the attempt.

But MacMillan was stubborn and daring. He flew on anyway, but not very far—not even to his next port of call. A balky engine twice forced him down onto the Bay of Bengal, the second time far from shore. Within two hours the leaky pontoon filled enough to upset the seaplane. MacMillan and his mechanic were rescued after three torturous days under the broiling sun afloat on the upside-down plane wreckage.

Other world flight attempts, including several at the time of the American effort, also failed due to technical problems. The Americans were not exceptionally lucky: Pontoons and struts broke and engines burned out, but these fliers were generally able to cope because they benefitted from "The Plan." The U.S. Army, heavily assisted by the navy and Coast Guard, had planned and laid out a massive support organization for the world fliers. Its teamwork in action gave the vital edge of success to the United States crews.

CHAPTER TWO

General Patrick's Plan

The 1924 ancestor of today's large, independent United States Air Force was a small organization linked to the U.S. Army as its "Air Service." During World War I the Air Service had grown from a tiny experimental outfit to include nearly nine thousand pilots. But in the peacetime 1920s after the "war to end wars," the Air Service had shrunk by 90 percent and had to compete for a share of the smaller army budget allowed by President Coolidge.

Major General Mason Patrick, commander of the Air Service, was an career army general. He had been placed in command of the expanded Air Service in World War I, when it flew and fought over France's Western Front. The general's devotion to his adopted outfit led him to learn to fly creditably at the age of sixty.

Patrick's style was to speak precisely but softly. If the small, outsider Air Service was to get on in military affairs, it had to be by intelligent persuasion. He sought support for his Air Service by displaying it to the public. The press was always welcomed at Air Service bases and careful planning produced a series of newsworthy record flights.

Early on, a Martin bomber was sent out on the first "around-the-rim" flight along the borders of the continental United States. It took seventy-eight days, and there was newspaper copy about it all of that

General Mason Patrick: world flight planner

time. A group flight from New York reached Nome, Alaska (no airplane had ever flown to Alaska), and returned safely.

How high could the army fly? Forty thousand frostbitten feet in 1921. How long could a plane stay aloft? Pilots in a two-seater flew for thirty-seven hours and were refueled by a risky hose connection from a hovering refueling plane.

Then, on its third try, a large, enclosed-cabin Fokker T-2 single-engine monoplane flew nonstop in 1923 from New York to San Diego, California—twenty-six hours, fifty minutes, and three seconds.

General Patrick's Air Service dared to start planning to fly around the world. There was no one person in the Air Service who promoted the idea of a record-setting around-the-world flight. It was the general feeling that this should be the next step. Certainly foreign airmen were planning or making an attempt, and, already, at home, the U.S. Navy had sent a pioneering group flight across the Atlantic Ocean in 1919.

For this navy project, four multi-engined Curtiss flying boats were readied, but one was wrecked early on. Three set out to cross the sea by way of Newfoundland and the Azores Islands to Portugal, and then on up to England. Only one, the NC-4 commanded by navy flier Albert C. Read, made it all the way, the first aircraft to fly across the Atlantic. The achievement was helped by painstaking preparation. For example, a line of twenty-five destroyers at fifty-mile intervals stretched under the airplanes much of the way across the sea.

So why didn't the U.S. Navy undertake the globe-girdling flight? A great deal of the route would be over oceans or along the sea edges of continents. It was a natural for the navy, but they muffed the opportunity.

The potential of lighter-than-air craft, dirigibles, were then of great interest to the navy, and there was a project for a dirigible expedition to the North Pole. At the same time, there was a political scandal, involving profiteering at naval oil reserves at Teapot Dome, Wyoming, and elsewhere. These took navy time and interest.

Meanwhile, at the Air Service, the world flight idea gained the vital support of General Patrick. During 1923, he was fortunate in obtaining the approval of the secretary of war, and the president. With this top-level support, Patrick was able to gain promises of cooperation and material support from the navy, Coast Guard, and State Department. Achieving this in a time when interservice rivalry was intense was nearly as remarkable a feat as successfully carrying through the flight!

General Patrick's Plan

The first questions addressed by the Air Service's officers, picked by General Patrick to serve on the World Flight Committee, were how and where to begin. To date, all European round-the-world expeditions were planned to fly in an easterly direction, taking advantage of prevailing west-to-east tailwinds and good flying weather. But America was set in another section of the globe, with different weather conditions.

Also, since it was not expected that the army fliers would have aircraft that could easily span oceans, (there would be four planes, with hope that at least one, like the navy's NC-4, would get through) the flight route would get over the Pacific by following the North American and Asian continent edges by way of Alaska, the Aleutian and Kurile Islands chains, and on along Asia via Japan, to China. This North Pacific area, though providing shelter for short-hop flights, had perhaps the worst flying weather in the world.

At the opposite side of Eurasia, it was planned to cross the Atlantic in short stages: Scotland–Iceland–Greenland–Labrador, another route-stretch of foul weather.

In the Aleutians and Kuriles the best month, between winter's hopeless chill and summer's prevalent fog, was May, and in the Iceland/Greenland area, August. In order for the planes to be in both places at the right time, the committee decided the planes must fly west into the wind and leave the United States in April 1924.

The Air Service owned no aircraft suitable for this adventure. The committee consulted Lieutenant Erik Nelson, a pilot considered to be the best engineering officer in their service. He recommended a *navy* biplane bomber he'd seen in Norfolk, Virginia. It was heavy enough to lug torpedoes and fling them into an enemy fleet. Nelson thought its design could be changed to carry fuel instead of torpedoes. It was a pontoon plane, suited to the route from America to India. Surely it could have wheels crafted to be installed there for the overland stretch up to Great Britain.

This navy bomber was one of the first designs of Donald Douglas, a brilliant young aeronautical engineer, now in his own business. He had taken over a former movie studio in Santa Monica, California.

The designer Donald Douglas *(right)* on the wing of a Douglas World Cruiser with Erik Nelson

Lieutenant Nelson was sent out to work with Douglas. On August 1, 1923, General Patrick approved, in blueprint, the Douglas World Cruiser. Thereafter, it was up to Douglas and Nelson to build, test, and have ready these tough, reliable airplanes in time for the world flight's April departure.

Developing the route meant negotiations with twenty-two foreign nations. While this project was underway, the World Flight Committee turned to the support problem. It began by facing up to the basically frail makeup of all 1920s airplanes. They knew that no aircraft could fly around the world without frequent and, at some points, major repairs. Making certain that spare parts and tools would be at hand was one of the committee's most important goals.

There would be about fifty landing or stopover points on the global route. At important stops, there would be a supply depot with major parts, such as engines, pontoons, and struts. And at *every* stop a basic emergency kit would be laid by, for the planes themselves could not carry much beyond men and fuel. The contents of all supply boxes were numbered and packed according to a system. It was planned that a pilot memorizing the kit order could pick out a desired part in darkness. At the far-flung fuel and supply depots the inventory was vast and detailed. For example, Box #3 at Reykjavik, Iceland, contained, among much else: Nuts, castellated, aircraft—#10s (40), ¼" (50), 5/16" (40), ⅜" (40), 7/16" (15), ½" (10)."

Liberty engines would power the Douglas World Cruisers. The four-hundred-horsepower Liberty was America's major contribution to World War I's combat air operations. Like all engines of that era, the Liberty had its faults, but there was a large leftover inventory, (about twelve thousand), and in the military's penny-pinching 1920s they were to be *used,* not replaced. Seventy engines were rebuilt for world flight use. The best thirty-five were shipped, some to Douglas, most as backups to the global depots. It turned out that several would be badly needed, along with many other stocked parts. The support plan was vital to flight success.

The World Flight Committee, sitting in Washington, D.C., churned out paperwork—orders, requisitions. How did they ensure that their commands would be carried through; that a pilot arriving in Iceland and needing "Nuts, castellated, aircraft" would lay his hand on them? The committee divided the global flight into six divisions and made an Air Service officer responsible within each.

All the supplies had to be shipped to their distant and often obscure supply depots. The division officer arranged commercial sea shipment. If that was unavailable, he had to negotiate with the navy or Coast Guard to carry and deliver the world flight supplies. These supply officers did not operate from an office in Washington, D.C. Each became a weary globetrotter (not by air, but by surface transportation) in the course of fulfilling his duties.

He had to visit, often more than once, *every* landing place scheduled in his division and also look into emergency facilities between. He had to seek out and appoint responsible hosts for the fliers and verify that designated supplies had arrived and been stored. The maps

Without the advance officer's attention to supplies, the world flight would not have flown beyond Alaska.

and briefing notes he gathered would be inserted in the pilots' airways guidebook. The officer would coordinate with the navy so that its ships would be stationed at intervals along the coastal or overseas legs of the route. As a sort of advance man, he would, when possible, travel on the ground just ahead of the planes when they were in his region.

The division officer, in addition to possessing strong administrative ability, had to be charming and patient as well. Every locality demanded special arrangements. Sitka, Alaska's, requests were typical: The world fliers were asked to search out and circle over the Alaskan Pioneers Old Folks Home; they were invited to visit Sitka's totem poles; and they were not to say a word about Juneau, the town that took away Sitka's honor as capital of Alaska. Division officer Lieutenant Clayton Bissell (a wartime ace), listened sympathetically, as did his colleagues around the world, though most of the requests would not be approved in Washington.

The advance officers followed through reliably on all fronts, keeping the fliers well serviced on the ground so that they could continue on around in the air. They were as vital to the flight's success as the planners, the movers of supplies, and the ships at sea. It was a *team effort,* and at the head of the team were the air crews.

10

CHAPTER THREE

The Chosen Few

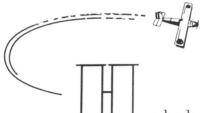

undreds of Air Service pilots applied for the job of handling a Douglas World Cruiser on the historic first great circle of the earth. Insiders who knew of the project early on attempted to get onto the World Flight Committee. That seemed just a step away from a world flier cockpit. As division officers, they hoped they might succeed a sick or injured flier in their area. But that never came about.

Formal application was to be accompanied by recommendation of the pilot's commanding officer, and about a hundred volunteered in this way. However, the world flight files include many letters from free-lance applicants. Many names that didn't achieve the four openings remain landmarks in today's USAF: Albrook, Brookley, Hickam, Lackland, MacDill, Spaatz, Tinker. Most of these future greats and heroes have had air bases named for them.

Lieutenant James Doolittle's letter is there in the world flight files. The future famous general and hero of "Thirty Seconds Over Tokyo" was coming along as one of the Air Service's finest pilots. But in this letter he probably "overshot his mission." Not stopping after listing his qualities, Doolittle laid out his own flight plan around the world. He wanted to use a Fokker cabin plane like the T-2 that had just crossed the USA nonstop. The applicant would hop across to

Hawaii (a first) and, via other Pacific islands, reach south Asia, then Europe, and fly nonstop back across the Atlantic. But Jimmy Doolittle was passed over for the world flight project.

As in many "open competitions," the final authority (General Patrick) had in advance a firm idea of whom he wanted. Patrick emphasized solid reliability as much as airborne navigational experience. "Solid" meant a low-profile officer on the ground (no cowboys!), for the world flight would also be a journey in diplomacy through many foreign nations.

First off, he certainly wanted Lieutenant Erik Nelson, the aircraft engineering professional and pilot who was overseeing the building of the Douglas World Cruisers.

Next he followed the recommendation of Major Henry "Hap" Arnold (who became the AAF's top commander in World War II) in picking Lieutenant Lowell Smith. Smith had made impressive long distance flights for the Air Service and was one of the thirty-seven-hour endurance fliers. Smith had also flown many hours over wilderness and mountains in western forest fire air patrols.

Lieutenant Leigh Wade was also chosen. Few in the Air Service had flown as many types of airplanes as Wade, a resourceful test pilot who daily confronted the aerial unknown. Lieutenant Wade also had a reputation as a fine air navigator.

Who shall be the world flight commander? General Patrick would have liked that for himself, but he was too old. So he chose an old army friend whom he knew would carry through. Though Major Frederick Martin had learned to fly just three years before, he had, by 1924, accumulated about seven hundred flying hours and had become a respected air base commanding officer. Martin, forty-two, looked and acted like the authority figure General Patrick wanted leading his Air Service fliers as they toured the world.

Two other pilots, Lieutenants Leslie Arnold and LeClaire Schulze, were chosen as reserves. Early in the New Year, the chosen flying officers attended a six-week world orientation class, where they were taught by experts in air navigation, map reading, route facts, weather, and medicine. The land-based airmen also needed to

In this official preflight pose are five of the World Fliers. They are left to right: Lieutenants Erik Nelson and Leigh Wade, Major Frederick Martin, and Lieutenants Leslie Arnold and Lowell Smith.

become skilled in pontoon takeoffs and landings. The navy coached them in these areas, while their colleague, Nelson, was on hand with the original Douglas World Cruiser to describe and demonstrate its characteristics.

A group of the Air Service's finest airplane mechanics worked with the world fliers. After observing them, each pilot chose his flying crewman. Here are the world flight's final air crews in their numbered planes named for American cities in the four compass directions:

1 *Seattle*

Major Frederick Martin, *pilot*
Sergeant Alva Harvey, *mechanician*

MAJOR MARTIN, forty-two, made the army his career from 1908 after graduating from Purdue University. He transferred from the Coast Artillery into the Air Service, with duty as a supply officer in France during the war. Though it was thought that it was best to learn to fly when young, Martin had gained his wings when he was pushing forty. The only family man among the fliers, he brought stability and an easy command style as leader of the global venture.

SERGEANT HARVEY, a twenty-three-year-old out of Cleburne, Texas, had joined the army as a teenager. Martin chose Harvey as his mechanician after judging him a steady, sturdy young man, who already had five years of service and who was a fine airplane mechanic.

Airmen of the *Seattle:*
Major Frederick Martin
and Sergeant Alva Harvey

Airmen of the *Chicago:* Lieutenants Leslie Arnold and Lowell Smith

 Chicago

Lieutenant Lowell Smith, *pilot*
Lieutenant Leslie Arnold, *mechanician*

LIEUTENANT SMITH, thirty-two, a minister's son from San Fernando, California, was an extraordinarily quiet individual who held his emotions in check. Yet, he had looked for adventure after college. Young Smith drifted from job to job across the U.S. southwest, relying on a natural mechanical ability, and then went south of the border. In patriot/bandit Pancho Villa's Mexican revolution Smith was the self-taught "engineering officer," caring for Villa's three-plane air force. But not for long: One by two by three, Smith watched them crash because of pilot errors or enemy fire. The adventurer returned to the States and a job at a silver mine.

Smith enlisted in pilot training when the Air Service expanded in World War I. He was a natural flier, and his superiors kept him in the U.S. as an instructor. When he finally reached France as a bomber pilot, the war was over. He stayed on in the Air Service and amassed fifteen hundred hours of flying time.

LIEUTENANT ARNOLD, twenty-nine, provided a personality balance on board the *Chicago*. Arnold, a personable native of New Haven, Connecticut, excelled on the playing field and in the number of trips to the principal's office. Out of high school, he talked his way into drama, touring New England with a summer stock acting company. Then he switched from acting to selling, becoming for a time a traveling salesman. He was working for a Connecticut submarine builder when he took the opportunity for Air Service pilot training.

Arnold also arrived in France too late for war action. He did his flying over Germany with the American occupation force. Continuing as an Air Service pilot in the States, he was assigned to promote his outfit by stunting at county fairs.

Arnold was at Seattle as first world flier back-up pilot when he was chosen by Smith to replace the *Chicago's* original sergeant mechanic, who had become ill near the departure date.

 Boston
Lieutenant Leigh Wade, *pilot*
Sergeant Henry Ogden, *mechanician*

LIEUTENANT WADE, twenty-eight, was born and raised on a farm near Cassopolis, a town not far from Kalamazoo, in the southwest corner of Michigan. In high school, young Wade excelled in sports and mathematics. He was planning to become a doctor when he went out to North Dakota to work the wheat harvest. Shortly thereafter, Wade joined the Michigan National Guard outfit that was called into federal service and sent down to relieve trouble on the Mexican border.

In 1917, seeking to become an officer, Wade went into U.S. Air Service pilot training in Canada. There he "learned to fly as naturally as a young bird." For a time, he was a flying instructor at Texas air

Airmen of the *Boston:*
Lieutenants Henry Ogden
and Leigh Wade

fields; he then went to France where he taught U.S. pilots aerobatic tactics. Wade's duties were then extended to testing aircraft supplied by France to the Air Service. By the time he came home after the war, Wade had likely piloted every type of airplane in Europe. In the peacetime Air Service, he continued testing new aircraft, aerial navigation aids, and high altitude flying.

SERGEANT OGDEN, twenty-three, grew up on a plantation in deep south Mississippi near Woodville. Too young for wartime duty, Ogden joined the Air Service as a private in 1919. He saw his first airplane when he was assigned to air mechanic school. The young airman was a natural mechanic and emerged as an instructor in the school. When engineer-minded Lieutenant Nelson conducted tough oral examinations among the mechanics at the world flight school, Ogden was one of the winners. He said he had come a long way from "manicuring cows along the Mississippi."

4 New Orleans

Lieutenant Erik Nelson, *pilot*
Lieutenant Jack Harding, *mechanician*

LIEUTENANT NELSON, thirty-five, born and raised in Sweden, inherited mechanical ability and the habit of attention to detail from his engineer father. Viking wanderlust was also in Nelson's blood. Following a happy childhood, he ran away to sea at sixteen. There were still merchant sailing ships then, and it was on these that the young man roamed the seven seas. Later he came to the United States seeking and finding a well-paid job on a rich man's yacht. At summer's end he went ashore and landed a job as mechanic and driver with a New York distributor of foreign automobiles. Employment on another yacht cruise left him in Florida, where he found work as the mechanic for a "flying fool," as the prewar exhibition pilots were known. This one went broke and didn't pay Nelson.

But the wandering Swede had been infected with airplane fever and yearned to be a flier. The closest he came was a job in the Curtiss aircraft factory. When World War I's pilot training opportunities opened, Nelson eagerly applied in the U.S. and Canada, but found his age (twenty-eight) a hindrance. Finally, he was accepted by the Air Service and became a fine pilot.

Nelson came naturally to long distance flying, while building his reputation for mechanical know-how, and he was chosen as chief engineer on the historic Alaska flight. Nelson already achieved *one* first among the world flight pilots: He had already gone around the world—under sail!

LIEUTENANT HARDING, twenty-seven, was a pleasant-mannered ("Smilin' Jack") mechanician out of Nashville, Tennessee. He studied mechanical engineering at Vanderbilt University, later working as test driver and mechanic for Detroit auto manufacturers. Although he entered the wartime Air Service as a private, his mechanical ability eventually raised his rank to master sergeant. Harding became the flying mechanic aboard the seventy-eight-day "round-the-rim" flight

Airmen of the *New Orleans:*
Lieutenants Jack Harding
and Erik Nelson

in 1919. In 1921, he exchanged sergeant stripes for a reserve lieutenant's commission and continued as a top level Air Service civilian employee.

Engineering perfectionist Nelson went to maximum effort to obtain Harding, in whom he saw mechanical ability of a high order. The Air Service at first refused to okay Harding, saying that only active duty personnel should get these prize appointments. But Major Martin backed Nelson and intervened with his friend General Patrick. Lieutenant Harding was selected.

With school and the selection process completed, it was time for the air crews to go to the Douglas plant and collect their airplanes as they came out of the factory. Four had been built, plus the original plane was in reserve. The Douglas World Cruisers were designed and constructed to be strong and tough. Here are aircraft details:

19

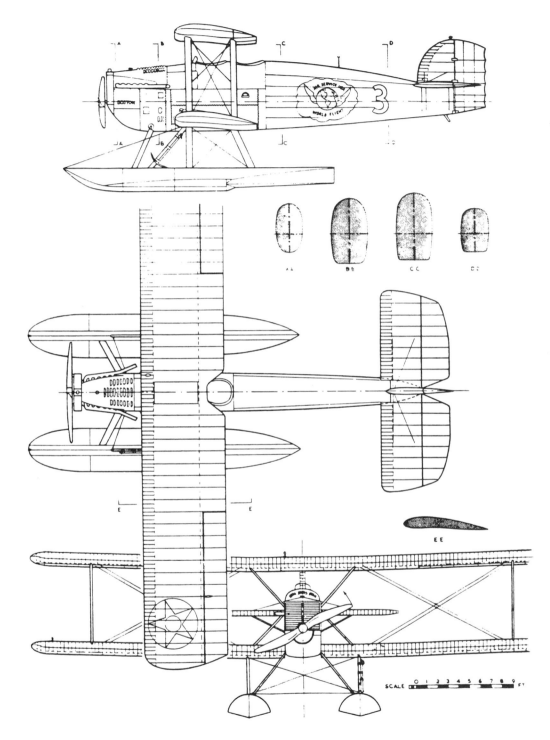

Scale Plan of the Douglas World Cruiser

Dimensions of the big biplanes with two roomy cockpits (pilot's up front): wing span fifty feet; height thirteen feet seven inches; length thirty-five feet six inches. The plane's empty weight was 4,300 pounds on wheels; 5,500 pounds on pontoons. The DWC carried maximum useful weight of 2,615 pounds, much of it gasoline, a maximum 450 gallons giving a flying range of about eighteen hundred miles.

The DWC's wings were of standard wood box beam and rib construction; but the fuselage was a new American design in tubular steel in three detachable sections. Varnished linen fabric enclosed the airplane.

The rejuvenated Liberty engine was primed to deliver about 420 horsepower to propel the plane to a top speed of just over one hundred miles per hour. Maximum ceiling (altitude) was modest—seven thousand feet with floats, ten thousand feet with wheels. They'd best stay out of the mountains! No stunt plane, the DWC climbed sluggishly at fifty feet per minute, landed at fifty-three miles per hour.

Women sew the canvas cover on the fuselage at the Douglas plant.

In the pilot's cockpit, control was maintained by means of a wheel grip attached to the "stick" by which all directional controls (flaps, elevator) were guided, except for the rudder, which was moved by right- and left-foot pedal bars. Cockpit instruments included compasses, air speedometer, altimeter (height gauge), bank-and-turn indicators (vital to comprehend angles of flight when flying blind), tachometer (engine performance), and water and oil gauges monitoring pressure and temperatures.

The early aircraft radio was available but was not installed, to save useful weight. The four expected to fly as a group, keep visual contact, and depend on hand signals. The cushions the crew sat on were floatable, but no life jackets or other sea survival gear was carried. No parachutes either. In whatever emergency, it was believed wisest to "stay with the plane," and without parachutes they would have to. The troubles that appeared as the crews broke in the new planes turned up principally in the Liberty engines, and were fairly easily solved.

The air crews lived in a Hollywood hotel, but did not "go Hollywood" to any extent. They were busy with preparations and attended few social functions. General Patrick kept an eye on them from Washington, and Major Martin would soon be writing to the World Flight Committee, "We will be very thankful and happy when the flight leaves Seattle with the noses of the planes pointed ever westward."

CHAPTER FOUR

North by Northwest

So anxious were Major Martin and his superiors to move out the world fliers on their beginning north-by-northwest flight plan that they set out for Seattle before the fourth plane was ready. On that morning of March 17, the cloud-blanketed northern mountain rim above Los Angeles caused the crews concern because it rose to around eight thousand feet. Smith knew the area well from his forest patrolling and assured Martin he could lead them into the north/south pass all aircraft used. So at 9:30 A.M. the *Seattle, Chicago,* and *Boston* roared up from Clover Field, Santa Monica, leaving the day-old *New Orleans* to follow soon. Ten planes carrying reporters and movie cameramen accompanied them through the forty-five hundred-foot Tehachapi Pass out into sunny brilliance over the San Joaquin Valley. There the first unscheduled landing (heralding the future) occurred when Martin landed the *Seattle* briefly for adjustments. The three world fliers made it into Sacramento, California, for their first night stopover.

In the morning the trio departed for Eugene, Oregon, and soon the *Boston* was fuming and spitting, a result of the radiator drain cap's vibrating open. In getting down fast to save his engine, Wade wiped off his tail skid. The *Seattle* and *Chicago* winged on into Eugene while other planes landed beside the *Boston* and assisted at its repair. Wade

23

Major Martin's *Seattle* at Clover Field, Santa Monica, before flying up the coast to the official start from Seattle

soon followed his comrades into Eugene. A short hop in the morning to Vancouver, Washington, was uneventful for the trio, but an accompanying press plane crashed in the Cascade Mountains.

In the morning the world fliers found a thick barrier of cloud and drizzle over the mountains between them and Seattle. Down they went "on the deck," leapfrogging and fishtailing close over the forested ridges, but they finally turned in the rainy gloom back to Vancouver. Meanwhile, Nelson, beginning his catch-up flights, piloted the *New Orleans* nonstop from Santa Monica to Eugene—a respectable eight hundred miles. The next day, Martin's threesome climbed above persistent fog banks and, using the clear-standing peaks of the northern Cascades—especially Mount Rainier—as guideposts, navigated over Seattle and edged down through the soup to land at the Sand Point airfield. The *New Orleans* roared in just half an hour later. The "Magellans" were poised for the true start of their aerial voyage.

Timing was the reason Washington, D.C., wasn't chosen as the great circle flight's starting place. President Coolidge and friends, the members of Congress, generals and admirals would have given the four crews a glittery send-off. But it was important to get over the Pacific during "good weather," and the detour from California to the capital and back out to Seattle might take ten days. Also, General Patrick's World Flight Committee was concerned with expenses. Probably they were having what we now call a "cost overrun."

Seattle's Sand Point Airfield lay beside Lake Washington, a very handy location for changing the DWCs from wheels to pontoons. And though they were not equipped with parachutes, the planes were now stocked with survival equipment including firearms, fishing gear, concentrated food packs, and sixty-pound anchors with 150 feet of line. For Air Service publicity, Seattle ladies christened each plane with a bottle of *water* (this was the era of Prohibition) taken up in the aircraft's home city.

The fliers were ready on April 4, but the weather was terrible. Early on April 5, Major Martin revved up the *Seattle,* and in charging across the lake broke his propeller and punctured a pontoon. Very embarrassing. All was repaired and ready on the morning of April 6.

North by Northwest

The *Seattle* again led out and off, followed by the *Chicago* and *New Orleans.* Meanwhile, Wade, in the *Boston,* could not rise from the water; the plane was too heavy. How embarrassing! Wade and Ogden pitched equipment from the tail locker helter-skelter, then tried again and got off.

Up ahead, the press planes dipped wings in farewell to the forward fliers. They were going where no one had flown before. The betting among aviation enthusiasts was that none, or perhaps only one, of the DWCs would complete the flight around the world. Across the globe, A. Stuart MacLaren had started out from England with his crew in a lone Vickers flying boat on an eastward course toward south Asia. There, perhaps, the two national teams would meet if their luck held.

After a low pass over his hometown of Bellingham, Washington, Major Martin led on up the Strait of Georgia between Vancouver Island and the mountainous Canadian mainland, bound for the day's destination harbor at Prince Rupert, British Columbia. They flew into haze that thickened into fog, forcing the three planes lower and lower till the DWCs faded from one another's sight. Skimming the glassy sea at seventy-five miles per hour, the pilots had to stand up to better

The route from Seattle to India was over water, so pontoons were installed.

gauge the thin line between mist and water. Compass bearings were their guide, confirmed by glimpses of landmarks.

Occasionally, the bulk and masts of fishing boats loomed at eye level and had to be dodged. And sometimes one airplane would run afoul of the propeller blast of another flying invisibly just ahead. When that happened, only the firmest control could prevent their being spun onto the sea surface. A break in the fog helped them avoid a large ferry.

The fog abated and was replaced with rain and snow squalls with open patches between. The sea surface roughened as they emerged into full exposure to the North Pacific, rolling in "forty-foot" waves.

At 4:55 P.M., after 650 hectic miles, Martin saw Prince Rupert and slanted the *Seattle* toward the harbor just as a dense snowstorm whipped in. Martin knew that this harbor was framed by steep wooded ridges, and he wanted to get down quickly before he smashed into one of the unseen hillsides. He groped the *Seattle* down in the snowy whiteout to where he judged the surface to be, but he was high by ten to thirty feet. The plane stalled (lost lift because of slowed forward motion), slid off sideways, and smacked heavily onto the bay. Luckily, the plane survived, but the impact damage to the left wing and pontoon made the *Seattle* a sorry sight. It is recorded that Major Martin here flung overboard the rabbit's foot a stateside well-wisher had given him.

The *Chicago* and *New Orleans* landed with due caution and were soon joined by the *Boston*, which navigator Wade had directed over a slightly shorter route. The mayor met them on the snowy dock, proclaiming the weather to be the nastiest in years. And after determining that the *Seattle* was repairable, the weary fliers called it a day—day one, with 170 to go!

Prince Rupert's business was shipping lumber, so port facilities were excellent and the *Seattle* was hoisted ashore for its repair. Local craftsmen were able to shape native spruce wood to restore broken or warped struts and supports. The fliers were impressed by the technical equipment—wiring, fasteners, tools—in the supply cache that advance officer Clayton Bissell had laid in. A day and a night's work "spruced up" the *Seattle* good as new. Meanwhile, Wade, routinely checking

Viking sailor Nelson saves the *Boston* and *New Orleans* from a collision in the surf at Sitka, Alaska, in this painting, one of a series, by Robert Sherry.

over his *Boston,* laid aside its cowling, the engine cover, and watched it slip in and sink in sixty feet of water! There wasn't another in stock, so a local coppersmith rapped out a replacement, making *Boston*'s nose distinctive in dark orange amid its pale aluminum-nosed fellows.

The weather lay low and foul over Prince Rupert, and even though visibility improved, it was still raining on April 10 when the American airmen departed. Major Martin's plan to rotate the flight leader set Smith and Arnold in the *Chicago* out front. As they entered Alaska's waterways, the oppressive cloud layers forced them to pass Ketchikan at fifty feet altitude. The salmon cannery wharves there were thick with cheering citizens.

Their destination was Sitka at 325 miles, and the flying was routine until Smith, to save seventy-five miles, tried to short-cut up a pass crossing an island. A lowering fog bank forced them toward treetops, so the *Chicago* banked tightly to turn back. The others followed in the cramped corridor, but the *Boston* got into a propeller wash and was nearly upset at twenty-five feet above the rocks. Their eventual arrival in Sitka was celebrated by a rare occurrence—fair skies.

Martin and company found Sitka, the capital of Alaska when the Russians settled it a hundred years before, to be quaint and pretty, "an arctic fairyland" according to Wade. But Sitka Sound is not well protected, as there are no barrier islands along its coast. A gale coming in erased the plan of next morning departure, and by noon the storm had torn the *Boston* from its mooring and had set it drifting toward the *New Orleans.* A collision would wipe out half the expedition!

The air crews rallied to the danger, and fortunately, a government Forestry Service launch, the *Ranger,* bounced over and got a restraining line onto the *Boston.* But the wind was fierce and the launch could not quite cope. It looked like destruction for the planes, but then Nelson took over. He waded out and boarded the *Ranger.* Shouting, the ex-Viking seaman took command of the ship, and the *Boston* was dragged back after coming within two feet of the *New Orleans.*

In the morning, there was still a heaving sea, but the mechanicians got out to look over the seaplanes. Nelson was strolling toward Sitka's post office when he saw that his *New Orleans* had come loose and was drifting toward the rocky beach. Yelling, he ran into the sea and was joined at neck level in the icy water by Smith. The pair were braced to try to fend off the four-ton DWC, when Harding, on board, succeeded in starting the *New Orleans'* engine and taxied away, saving the plane, if not tempers!

The world fliers escaped from Sitka the next morning, led by Wade and Ogden in the *Boston* on a flight of 625 miles to Seward. They were plagued by fog again and spent much time zipping along below the weather, following the wavering line of surf and beach. On this trip they abandoned tight formation when flying in low visibility, because of the dangers. There was spectacular glacier scenery close at hand on the right, when they could see it. Nelson said that he could feel the coldness of the massed ice cliffs on his cheeks when the *New Orleans* passed very near in the gray blankness of fog.

The railhead port of Seward also lived on salmon, with the seasonal harvest just then beginning. Since it snowed heavily the next day, the air crews had a bit of time to mingle with the colorful, rough and ready characters working the salmon run. Seward also introduced them to a weather character—the williwaw—which would make their lives miserable for weeks to come.

The "woolies," as Arnold and others called them, were small, devilish storms that unpredictably whirled or blasted down onto the sea from the icy mountains. The locally destructive winds wandering this way and that, could in a minute or two raise a mighty sheet of water or, coming ashore, scatter a lumber pile like straws. The fliers borrowed heavy ropes and anchors and tied the four DWCs close behind a cannery pier.

On April 15, the group got away, turning west for Chignik, 425 miles out toward the tip of the Alaskan peninsula, where the bleak chain of Aleutian Islands begins. Nelson and Harding, in the *New*

Mechanics do maintenance on a Douglas World Cruiser.

Orleans, led and immediately had to circle awhile, for the *Seattle* was tardy in getting off. Airborne, it lagged behind and below. Nelson occasionally slowed to allow Martin to catch up. The major did not, however, signal any difficulty.

The fliers' attention was taken on their right by mighty Mount Katmai, a split-open mountain which had erupted in 1912. The fliers glimpsed the volcanic vapors rising from the nearby Valley of Ten Thousand Smokes, and then flew into a series of snow squalls. In the clear again, they looked back for the *Seattle.* Their comrade did not appear, and in time they knew that Martin and Harvey had gone down somewhere in this absolute wilderness.

Because the DWCs had been bucking a stiff headwind all day, fuel was a foremost consideration. They could not linger to search without the likelihood that they would run out of fuel and have to come down at sea on some forbidding coast. Instead, Nelson and the others put on all speed over the final hundred miles into Chignik, where they knew a radio station had been established for their benefit.

After the 4:25 P.M. landing, Smith ordered the radio operator to SOS on the *Seattle*'s behalf. Here the careful preparations of the distant but wise World Flight Committee showed to good advantage. Two navy destroyers, the *Hull* and the *Cory,* were in the area. Closer but slower was the *Haida,* a Coast Guard cutter with advance officer Bissell aboard. Advised of probable location by Smith, Bissell, as officer responsible for the area, agreed that the western end of Shelikof Strait, and Portage and Wide Bays, would be searched from dawn onward. And from the *Hull* and the *Cory* crackled the message that they were proceeding to the scene at top speed of thirty-two knots.

CHAPTER FIVE

And Then There Were Three

Aboard the *Seattle*, the prospect of a forced landing became immediate when the oil pressure gauge sank to zero. Mechanician Harvey crawled forward on the wing root into the foul oil spray. He verified a leak that caused a total loss of lubricant. Down below, a forty-mile-an-hour wind roughened the sea but they were flying beside the coast and were able to land in sheltered Portage Bay. After the *Seattle* was anchored offshore, an unrepairable three-inch hole in the Liberty engine's crankcase was discovered. After munching a few malted milk tablets, Martin and Harvey spent a shivering, sleepless night in their cockpits.

Fortunately, the April dawn came early and fair. At 5:00 A.M. the marooned fliers saw a wisp of steamer smoke that grew into the profile of the destroyer *Hull*. Martin repeatedly fired their flare signal pistol. Finally, a launch picked them up, and the thoroughly chilled airmen enjoyed a hot breakfast aboard the *Hull*. The *Seattle* was placed in tow, and the ship steamed slowly to the nearest fishing village, Kanatak.

But Kanatak had no sheltering harbor, and Martin's greeting by the forty townsfolk included the remark that today was the first calm day they had seen in eight months! The plane was then towed up a creek into a pond offering safety from the sea. Meanwhile, radio

Major Martin wades in to break up ice floes threatening the *Seattle* in the creek at Kanatak.

messages dispatched the Coast Guard vessel *Algonquin* from Dutch Harbor, the Aleutians, with a replacement motor. Martin also messaged that the *Chicago, Boston,* and *New Orleans* were to fly on from Chignik to the supply base at Dutch Harbor.

The wind soon picked up at Kanatak, and though the sea could not lash the *Seattle,* it was now endangered by drifting pancake ice in the freshwater pond. Martin and Harvey had to wade repeatedly into the icy water to smash ice floes near the pontoons. Martin, weakened by exposure on Portage Bay, ended up in bed.

When the *Algonquin* arrived, the new Liberty engine was skillfully off-loaded into a whaleboat on the choppy sea, rowed ashore and up the creek. The *Algonquin*'s crew assisted in the heavy lifting of engine removal and replacement. Harvey and an *Algonquin* crewman worked all night by lantern light to install the new engine.

Meanwhile, gladly acting on Major Martin's order, the other world fliers got out of barren, two-cannery Chignik. Williwaws were skipping about and roughness on the bay resulted in mechanicians Arnold, Harding, and Ogden getting soaked while lying on pontoons to release their buoy ties. They then flew in their drafty open cockpits many chilling hours in wet clothing. The weather was fair, so Smith and Arnold, leading in the *Chicago*, were able to cut forty miles off the day's flight by shortcutting over a peninsula outside Chignik. The three planes arrived safely in Dutch Harbor and joined Lieutenant Bissell, their advance officer, in cozy quarters aboard the Coast Guard ship *Haida*.

The *Seattle* was finally ready to leave Kanatak. But a thirty-mile-per-hour wind ruffled the sea, and a snowstorm was approaching. What to do? Martin and Harvey went. The takeoff was the trickiest of the trip, and then they had to fly "on the deck," pilot talk for extreme low level flying, semiblind most of the way to Chignik, occasionally dodging looming cliffs or rocky isles close to the beach line. On one occasion, passenger Harvey likely saved the plane by a hard kick at a rudder pedal.

This hazardous journey occurred on April 25. That same day General Patrick messaged Bissell: "Where is Major Martin? British flight at Karachi." But now, in Chignik, it snowed for three days with exceptionally high winds. At anchor, the tossing *Seattle* became coated with an estimated four hundred pounds of ice sheathing. On the 29th, they were able to get out to the plane to remove the ice and prepare for flight on the morrow. Probably it was from Chignik that Major Martin wrote to the World Flight Committee, "We more nearly resemble longshoremen than members of the U.S. Air Service."

Martin and Harvey arose at three-thirty A.M. on April 30. Another dreary snowfall was occurring, but the wind was way down. Later in the morning the snow stopped, though it remained quite cloudy. The radio at Dutch Harbor reported passable weather. Martin decided to go, and he wanted to use the peninsula shortcut that Smith and Arnold had led the others through. The Chignik cannery superintendent pointed out, across the bay, its general direction.

The *Seattle* lifted off, and within minutes Martin and Harvey were flying up a level pass in a generally westerly direction. Suddenly, though, Martin had a mountain in his face! He turned back, and near the place on the coast where he had entered the pass he saw another pass branching low and level to the northward. He hoped this northerly direction of the pass was only temporary and guided the *Seattle* up the valley. The pass direction did not change, though, so Martin planned to return to the bay at Chignik and fly around the longer sea route to Dutch Harbor.

Then the pilot spied blue water away to the west. He pointed the *Seattle* toward it, "but somehow that body of water never got any nearer." Now a fog bank intervened, but Martin confidently climbed into it, expecting to emerge on top and continue west. But as the heavily loaded plane climbed sluggishly in the fog, the bare slope of a nearby mountain came dimly into sight, and seconds later the *Seattle* crashed!

Disaster it surely was, but at least they had not collided with a vertical cliff. The *Seattle* had plowed onto a gently ascending slope well padded with snow. It did not catch fire nor shatter into pieces, though its bottom wings and pontoon undercarriage were mangled. Martin sustained light facial cuts and Harvey no injury at all. But both dejectedly understood that their world flight had finished upon an unknown mountain somewhere on the backbone of the bleak Alaskan Peninsula.

This main east/west peninsula formed the narrow crest between the Pacific Ocean to the south, and the more frigid Bering Sea to the north. The fliers knew they had to get out on their own. No one could come in from the coasts to them. But a seamless union of dense white fog and snow prevented them from moving that afternoon. The pair floundered awhile in the deep snow, finding it difficult to maintain balance in the blank whiteness. They backtracked to the plane and spent a miserably cold night jammed into the rear fuselage of the *Seattle*.

On the second day, the fog remained impenetrable, so they stayed at plane-side. Their emergency supplies included containers of concentrated liquid food which, doled out a few spoonfuls a day, might last a week. They were able to shape snow blocks to enclose the edges of plane wreckage like an igloo. Shielded from the chilly night breezes, they rested more comfortably.

The alarm was raised all along the Alaskan peninsula's Pacific coast, for each salmon cannery had been primed to radio its report of hearing the planes passing. So it was known the *Seattle* disappeared near its start. Coast Guard vessels searched area coves on the Pacific side, and a dog team expedition searched over the shortcut that Martin and Harvey should have followed. The *Chicago, Boston,* and *New Orleans* remained at Dutch Harbor. They would have been of no use among the mountains into which it was now correctly feared the fliers had crashed. A newspaper syndicate posted a thousand-dollar reward.

The mists still lingered on Martin and Harvey's third day, but they decided to hike out. The temperature was above freezing in the daytime, so both shucked their leather flying suits as too cumbersome and, layered with ordinary clothing, followed a southward compass bearing into the fog, wanting very much to come down on the Pacific shore. They crossed the ravine of a stream head and climbed its far slope. At the top, the mist parted briefly and they saw that they were about to walk off a snow-covered cliff! Later, the cliff was estimated to have a fifteen-hundred-foot drop.

Now Martin decided to head downstream even though it appeared to be flowing toward the Bering Sea. Harvey became increasingly affected by snow blindness as they trudged down the valley

Major Martin and Sargeant Harvey leave the *Seattle* crash site to seek help in this Sherry painting.

hoping for a pass opening southward to appear. But they saw none, and at day's close, they came out on the edge of a broad marshy flat they could not cross. They made a makeshift overnight camp in an alder thicket.

The same day, May 2, a decision was made in far-off Washington, D.C., and transmitted by radio relay to Dutch Harbor:

LT. LOWELL SMITH

C.O. ROUND THE WORLD FLIGHT

DO NOT DELAY LONGER WAITING FOR MAJOR
MARTIN TO JOIN YOU. SEE EVERYTHING DONE
POSSIBLE TO FIND HIM. PLANES 2, 3, AND 4 TO
PROCEED JAPAN AT EARLIEST POSSIBLE MOMENT.

PATRICK

In the general's view, his world flight was getting into far-flung difficulties. The Alaskan delays and the missing flight commander were weakening the determined belief of all concerned that the project would be carried through to success.

Further delay would use up fuel on board the American destroyers stationed in Japan's northern Kurile Islands, and the ships might have to withdraw before the flight reached the area. Also, though the world flight program was not considered a "race," it would be a costly embarrassment to the Air Service if the British—now joined by French and Portuguese flights—were to complete the global circuit ahead of the Americans. So far, the other three national teams were flying well as they approached south Asia.

On May 3, the lost world fliers climbed back up the stream valley to the *Seattle* wreckage. Harvey's failed eyesight meant he practically had to be led. However, at the plane, application of an ointment in their medical kit cleared up the sufferer's vision remarkably. On May 4, visibility lifted a thousand or more feet, and the pair climbed to the top of their mountain for a look around.

To the south lay a deep canyon backed by a wall of taller mountains, their tops hidden in the persistent overcast. No hope that way. But to the west the mountainscape leveled down to a lake, and immediate hope was raised that some native or migrant trapper might live there. The rest of that day the fliers slogged toward it and again camped overnight in a thicket. But at least they dined well, for on the march they had shot two ptarmigans. This fowl, an arctic grouse, is quite tame in uninhabited areas.

The lake was reached by noon of the sixth day, but it turned out to be just another lonely wilderness sheet of water. They followed a stream exiting southwestward, but it soon turned north and the wanderers had to go on along beside it. Now Martin's eyesight required treatment; indeed, the middle-aged major approached exhaustion. At 2:00 P.M. the pair halted in a dry place with plentiful firewood, sipped a few spoonfuls of their dwindling food concentrate, and turned in after attending to the daily, vital chore of drying their socks.

Scouting to the sides in the morning, the more vigorous Harvey (twenty years younger than his superior) discovered a stream head starting south. They floundered along through deep snow beside this watercourse and quit in midafternoon when it also twisted north. Harvey, however, reported that the sea was about three miles ahead. Up at dawn, they reached the beach of a broad bay at 7:30 A.M. The numerous ice cakes afloat offshore meant that this was the remote Bering Sea. A half-expected disappointment. But their salvation immediately appeared in a sweep of Harvey's binoculars—a small cabin not far away!

Though unoccupied, the cabin seemed to have had recent use. It contained some food and household gear, including a rifle and ammunition. Martin and Harvey enjoyed a late breakfast of pancakes. Major Martin's eyesight had certainly improved, for he afterward shot two sitting ducks with the rifle, and Harvey brought back two snowshoe rabbits from an exploration hike. The ducks and rabbits, with pickled salmon, made up a feast prepared by a revived Martin. Then a savage blizzard enveloped their cozy shack, and they knew that had they not found this refuge neither would be alive.

After the storm, the weather improved. Looking down from nearby heights, they discovered that they were overlooking sizeable Port Moller Bay, and there were food cartons in the cabin from a cannery at the bay entrance. On May 10, a fair day, the lost fliers

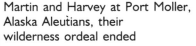

Martin and Harvey at Port Moller,
Alaska Aleutians, their
wilderness ordeal ended

undertook a wearing journey of about twenty-five miles along the beach and over many rock barriers jutting seaward. Because of the large amount of ice still in the bay, they feared the cannery might be locked and deserted. But when they came in sight of it, the weary companions were overjoyed to see smoke rising from its chimney, and they knew they were saved.

The men of the *Seattle* were welcomed and made comfortable, and word crackled from Port Moller's radio of their courageous survival. It happened that the vice-president of the cannery headquarters in the United States arrived soon after on the company's ship. Major Frederick Martin and Sergeant Alva Harvey were offered, and accepted, passage straight back to Seattle, and so they pass out of the world flight story.

40

CHAPTER SIX

West by Southwest

ieutenant Lowell Smith, the new flight commander, acted immediately on General Patrick's instructions to proceed toward Japan. The *Chicago, Boston,* and *New Orleans* got out of Dutch Harbor early on May 3, flying westward along the Aleutian chain of treeless, mountaintop islands to land in the harbor at Nazan, an Aleut native village on Atka Island.

The fliers' stay at Dutch Harbor, where they worriedly awaited the arrival of Major Martin and Sergeant Harvey, was wearing on their morale. However, they took advantage of the time at this major supply base to work on the three DWCs so that they were in good-as-new shape for the rugged stretch ahead to Japan. The *Boston* received a new engine, the second for this plane since leaving Santa Monica.

Weather was the critical factor in the Aleutians, though after enduring fogs and storms from Seattle to Dutch Harbor, the air crews might have wondered how much worse it could get. Fortunately, they had Major William Blair, the Air Service's crack weatherman, to sail ahead along the route and radio back weather commentary. The weatherman was now aboard the *Eider,* a small Coast Guard cutter bobbing in choppy seas off Attu Island at the end of the Aleutian chain and America. Blair could only forecast, not make, weather, so the world flight was held up six days at Atka.

The *Boston* receives another new engine at Dutch Harbor, in the Alaska Aleutians.

The air crews lived indoors, but in primitive conditions, with most of them sleeping on the floor. Commander Smith did their cooking; "Eggs Viennese" three times a day, according to Nelson, though he confides they finagled two chickens for one good meal. The eighty local Aleuts were unhelpful. A visit by men from the sky did not impress them. The once-thriving Aleut tribe of fishermen and seal hunters had been nearly extinguished by a century's contact with white explorers.

Williwaws and their by-products kept the crews vigilant and active in protecting their tossing seaplanes. Harding and Ogden, out servicing lanterns on the DWCs, became castaways when a whirl of wind blew their rowboat away and smashed it in the darkness onto a rocky shore. They emerged from neck-deep water to hike back in a driving rainstorm. Fishing and hunting filled out some days. Out on an eagle hunt (Arnold wrote in his diary), the hunters were lucky not to have shot each other in their clumsy enthusiasm.

At last, on May 9, came a fly-ahead signal from Major Blair at Attu. As they were taking off, a crosswind had to be handled, and just before the *New Orleans* reached flying speed, Nelson saw that a williwaw had unpredictably arisen, roiling the sea, blowing in from one side on a collision course with the plane. Slowing and turning a bulky seaplane speeding at about eighty miles per hour was not easy nor safe, but pilot skill and a solid airplane managed it. Nelson got off on the second try.

Often out of sight of land on this day's trip, the fliers saw little of note except treacherous whirlpools formed below by the meeting of the separate tides from the Arctic and Pacific Oceans—not an invitation to a forced landing. As their next aerial leap was to span the North Pacific, the fliers were pleased to find their compasses in fine condition. When their day's destination came into sight, Arnold noted in his diary that, "Attu Island looks like the end of everything. . . . beyond lies Asia."

Attu had an even smaller and humbler Aleut settlement, but the fliers were at first able to bunk with the Coast Guard on the *Eider.*

DWCs of the round-the-world flight sheltering ashore for fear of the williwaws

Their old refuge, the *Haida,* also arrived, but was unable to enter the shallow bay, and a storm blew the vessel well out to sea. On Attu, the reassuring news of Martin's and Harvey's escape reached their old companions. An English officer acting as advance arranger for the British team had recently stocked Attu and left the Americans an encouraging message. Still the weather continued Aleutian, "two kinds . . . bad and worse," according to Arnold. They did not get their chance to hop the Pacific till May 15.

This historic first aerial crossing of the Pacific Ocean was planned as an 870-mile trip from Attu to Paramushiru Island, the northernmost acceptable destination in Japan's Kuriles, a chain of mountainous islands (now controlled by the Soviet Union). About an hour out from Attu, the three aircraft passed low over the Coast Guard's *Haida,* "rolling and tossing about like a cork," with most of its crew of old friends "hanging on with one hand and waving good-bye to us with the other," in Smith's phrasing. Then, as they droned on southwest, a massive blue-bellied storm they could not enter loomed in their route path. So the trio turned aside on a northwest bearing toward the rock piles of the Kommandorski islands.

In seeking this haven, the fliers were confronting a continent-wide political obstruction—the Union of Soviet Socialist Republics. The Communist revolution had occurred almost seven years before, and the United States did not have official relations with the new Soviet government. This was a principal reason for the U.S. world flight path's bending southwest around the fringes of Asia. Much shorter (and used in 1933 by seven-day around-the-world flier Wiley Post, among others) would have been a direct westerly course across Siberia to Moscow and on across northern Europe.

The few Russians residing on these barren isles six thousand miles from Moscow were not likely, Smith hoped, to come out shooting. So the Kommandorskis had been chosen as an emergency alternate stop, and the Coast Guard's little *Eider* was steaming nearby. Smith's superb navigational instinct was on the mark as he led through storm patches right to the small island group. Happily, visibility allowed their finding the *Eider* and sending a message to it. The ship moved in to three miles off the Soviet port village of Nikolski. The DWCs landed successfully in mildly rough seas and were attached to buoys dropped from the *Eider*. It had been a five-hour daytime flight, but the day had changed from May 15 to 16 beyond the International Date Line where tomorrow is born.

Immediately, a boat bearing five Russians came out from the village and a conference followed aboard the *Eider*. Luckily, a sailor was able to speak English and Russian, so that it was explained the visit was because of weather emergency and would be as brief as possible. The men of the Kommandorskis were courteous but asked that the Americans not come ashore. Later they sent out a flagon of vodka (not consumed by the fliers). The morning dawned fair, and at 4:30, refueling from the *Eider* and other preparations were finished. The DWCs were at the point of leaving when the bearded committee came out again and told them Moscow had messaged, ordering the Americans to leave. Just move your boat aside, said Smith, and we will.

The Americans flew straight over (150 miles) to Siberia, to make use of the giant snowy caps of the line of volcanoes along its Kamchatka Peninsula as navigation markers. Their grandeur lay on the right as a fleecy cloud bank gathered beneath and the pilots flew on south via the peaks. Later the weather worsened at all altitudes and, when the crews were sure they were over the coastal sea, the trio went down to fly once again on the deck until they sighted Paramushiru. The *Chicago, Boston,* and *New Orleans* landed in V formation on the bay at 11:37 on May 17, 1924. They had overcome the Pacific for aviation!

When word of the world fliers' arrival on the other side of the Pacific reached the *Haida*, Lieutenant Bissell was finally relieved of responsibility, though its pressures had been most intense during the ten days the men of the *Seattle* were missing. His superiors later rewarded Bissell's conduct by appointing him advance officer for the U.S. reception when the fliers had circumnavigated the globe.

Japan was the principal concern of Lieutenant Clifford Nutt, advance officer of the second division. He needed to spend practically all his time attending to relations with the Japanese government in

Tokyo. Two conditions made the world flight negotiations delicate there:

Japan had embarked upon a warlike course of expansion in the Pacific, which increasingly upset American interests in the region. So its military was suspicious of U.S. reasons for flying over Japan. And in the United States, the large number of Japanese immigrants had aroused fear and suspicion in the western states. As a result, Congress was passing a law to exclude new Japanese immigration and to deny U.S. citizenship to those already resident. That Japan allowed the world fliers to cross its territory from end to end, and to tolerate the U.S. Navy's presence in its northern waters, was a triumph for American diplomacy.

The U.S. destroyers *John D. Ford* and *Pope* had been on station in the Kurile Islands (and watched by three Japanese destroyers) since the middle of April. They had found the harbors partially blocked by floating ice then; but several tedious and dangerous weeks had passed before the three planes finally attempted the Pacific crossing. Meanwhile, in the Kuriles, the wind blew in successive storms that mounted to the force of arctic hurricanes. Only superb seamanship and luck saved the United States from the loss of the *Ford* and the *Pope* at sea or on a mountainous Japanese coast.

The two-day storm that began on May 8 at Paramushiru was the worst. Foreign correspondent Linton Wells, aboard the *Pope,* reported:

> Picture the scene: Three destroyers—two Japanese, one American—are anchored in a shallow bight off a narrows which flows between two adjacent headlands into an ocean of mountainous waves. The wind strikes at these vessels with a velocity of more than one hundred miles an hour. . . . Their anchors drag. They roll steadily from side to side— twenty, twenty-five, thirty degrees each way from the vertical. To put to sea would probably mean disaster, so their skippers attempt to keep them where they are.

Time and again the *Pope,* dragging anchors, was blown across the bay and had to advance its engines to plow back and resume position. Then, in the night, the gale overwhelmed its guidance, and the *Pope* drifted swiftly toward the Japanese destroyer *Tokitsukaze.* Engines rumbled on the *Pope,* and the helmsman threw the wheel hard over! Sideways, the *Pope* glanced against the *Tokitsukaze,* raking a long scar aft before slipping past into the stormy darkness with its dented prow. Another day and night of hundred-mile-per-hour winds, of near-miraculous survival, passed before the weather calmed. Wells surveyed the deck:

> I stood on the bridge and in the dim light gazed upon a remarkable picture: the destroyer's deck was littered with the debris of wrecked boats, practically every square inch of paint had been blown off, and, believe it or not, the four smokestacks were covered with a thick layer of ice—and two of the stacks were in use and steaming hot! Which indicates how cold and how strong was the wind.

All aboard agreed they would never see the world fliers in this stormy environment. So, when the three planes abruptly dodged out from beneath a snow-laden cloud, the men aboard the *Pope* (and the Japanese, too) reacted in joyful disbelief at seeing their long, punishing wait so rewarded!

Slipping into Paramushiru, the *Chicago, Boston,* and *New Orleans* had caught the Kuriles' weather dragon napping, but the same evening an ordinary gale arose, which came, according to the *Boston's* Wade, within a half hour of wrecking the expedition by pounding into shreds the lines securing the DWCs. It was worse than the williwaws. The pilots yearned to fly south! Just another thousand miles, and all would be balmy.

May 19, on the coldest trip yet, the world flight reached Yeterofuru Island, 595 miles southwest, at the base of the Kuriles island chain. En route, the curious airmen swooped to look into the smoking craters of several volcanoes, the only hot spots on these islands.

On May 22, they flew 485 miles down to Miniato on the main Japanese island of Honshu. Trees, agriculture, towns, civilization! About three thousand well-wishers gathered at Miniato to entertain the fliers from across the Pacific. But Miniato's port was too open to the sea, the wind too brisk; so the flight departed as soon as refueling was done. Lieutenant Nutt had come up from Tokyo, and the advance officer was left to earn his pay by explaining the fliers' seeming discourtesy.

For the next 350 miles a storybook Japanese landscape passed below their wings. The crews believed that each village was alerted, and their journey became a wave parade. The landed at the Japanese military seaplane base on Lake Kasumigaura, near Tokyo. In reaching Tokyo they closed the last unflown gap in the world's circuit, for the route onward to Europe had been flown (mostly *from* the west) by others; and a few intrepid airmen had already ventured to fly between Europe and North America.

CHAPTER SEVEN

Jungle Adventure of the *Chicago*

The social side of being famous fliers circling the globe, heroes in the making, with whom local big shots expected to hobnob and whom ordinary folk flocked to see, was first evidenced in Japan. It was an additional duty, at once embarrassing, gratifying, and boring. There wasn't much open time in the airmen's schedule: Up before dawn, wait for the weather, fly several often-tense hours, and afterward undertake hours of aircraft care. The Liberty engine needed a good deal of attention, and generally, Arnold remarks, "Always on an airplane there is something to be done—not something imperative to be done right away, but better to do it than leave undone."

That attitude had been impressed on them by Nelson. Their engineering specialist understood how chancy aircraft technology was in 1924. So he taught the crew to keep the world flight planes in top shape mechanically. This was each crew's responsibility, for other hands seldom touched the DWCs, and not without their air crews' presence. As a result, the welcoming committee of the day might be kept waiting for hours; and if a late festive dinner lingered on, and one head or several were seen to nod toward sleep, it was a natural outcome.

Flight Commander Smith's confidence dried up at his social duties ashore. He was no glad-hander or after-dinner speaker. Smith's opening remarks were next to his closing words. Grinning, he'd remark they didn't care to be "Magellans of the air" because Magellan didn't survive his journey. But then, Smith would become tonguetied. So it was fortunate for the flight commander to have at his side his personable *Chicago* companion, Arnold, whose ease in public speaking came out of his past acting experience.

The American record-setters were admirably hosted wherever they passed in Japan, a remarkable occurrence at this time when President Coolidge had signed the law excluding Japanese from

Leslie Arnold deals with civil ceremonies in Japan.

America and their own General Billy Mitchell had made the prediction that the United States and Japan would eventually be at war, so it would be best for the U.S. to get on with its preparations for it. Though the governing class was stung by these events and withheld welcome, the traditional Japanese courtesy to guests shielded the fliers.

While spending two days at pure public relations in Tokyo, the American team became well acquainted with Colonel L. E. Broome, the advance man for the rival English world flight. They got along because they had so much in common: Both had survived Alaska, the Aleutians, and Kuriles at about the same time. During this friendship came a dread radiogram reporting that the MacLaren plane was wrecked beyond repair, though the crew survived, at Akyab on the coast of Burma. Colonel Broome gestured despondently, remarking, "Two years' work gone west."

But Smith knew that a spare English plane had been unloaded in a northern Japanese port. He volunteered to ask the U.S. Navy to have it transported to Akyab. The commander of the destroyer group attending the American flight consulted with his commanding admiral, who agreed. So a U.S. destroyer took aboard the crated aircraft and delivered it to Hong Kong where, since the British Navy declined to help MacLaren's private venture, another U.S. destroyer ferried the plane through typhoon-lashed seas to Akyab. It was, Broome declared, "the finest bit of sportsmanship I've ever heard of."

While at the Lake Kasumigara base, all three DWCs had new engines installed and were generally renovated for the tropics. Smith carried the Japanese naval air commander aloft on the test flight of the *Chicago,* an adept diplomatic gesture. Smith also wired an urgent recommendation to Washington and received General Patrick's reply, ordering that the mechanician on the *Boston* now be promoted to *Lieutenant* Henry Ogden.

On June 1, they were prepared to depart at dawn and were surprised to learn that a chartered train packed with Japanese officials had come out from Tokyo at that hour to see them depart. Their hosts recommended they watch for a view of Fujiyama. It was cloudy inland, but at the appropriate moment the world fliers saw the clouds part to the west to reveal the beautiful, artistically shaped cone of Japan's sacred 12,500-foot slumbering volcano, Fujiyama, "his snowy summit standing out against the cobalt sky . . . revealing himself to encourage and inspire us," wrote Arnold.

Soon the flight passed into foul weather. It was the typhoon season on the east Asian coasts, and the Americans promptly flew into the outskirts of one. When they arrived over Kushimoto harbor, halfway down Japan from Tokyo, below their wings lay the familiar *Pope*, again rolling in a storm. The seaplanes made a half-dozen exploratory landing approaches before skillfully getting down. There was difficulty in reaching and tying to the buoys dropped by the *Pope*, with the mechanicians washed by waves as they lay on the pontoons awaiting the opportunity to hook up.

In the morning it turned fair. So, breaking away from civic ceremonies ashore, the crews got off in the afternoon to fly onward to Kagoshima, a major port at the south end of Kyushu island and of Japan proper. Wade set the *Boston* down briefly en route to refill its radiator. The trio arrived together before about fifty thousand enthusiastic onlookers. Nearly half were school children who had been taught "My Country 'Tis of Thee" in English and they now sang it as they waved American and Japanese flags, a salute that greatly affected the U.S. fliers.

Because a 550-mile flight over the lower Yellow Sea now faced the fliers, the U.S. Navy deployed an arc of destroyers across it toward China to ease the danger of a forced landing far out to sea. On June 4, the *Boston* and *New Orleans* departed Kagoshima for Shanghai, China. The *Chicago* remained, temporarily defeated by the problem of takeoff from a very calm sea. The lack of waves on the water's surface increased the sea's static grip on the undersurface of the pontoons.

Calm water had been unknown in the north. Now Smith and Arnold ingeniously attacked this problem by taxiing the *Chicago* out at top speed, well ahead of the others. Utilizing the disturbed water, the *Boston* and *New Orleans* arose, while the *Chicago* swung about to use their wakes in turn. But it didn't work. The flight commander then signaled those aloft to continue, and he and Arnold spent time diving to inspect their pontoons and then to repair a loose stripping discovered on the underside of one float.

As they droned ahead for six hours, Nelson, of the *New Orleans*, thought about his time on the Yellow Sea as a young sailor on a tramp windjammer and mused on the advances in form and speed made in a dozen years. About forty miles off the China coast the sea's color shifted from deep blue to green and finally "to liquid gold in the sunlight," the result of soil discharged from the vast Yangstze River winding from the heartland of China. If the river was straightened and transposed upon the United States, it would stretch from coast to coast.

The DWCs alighted on a stretch of river cleared of its normal Shanghai traffic of thousands of small boats. Nelson had seen that, in the new, hot climate, the long exhaust stacks on the Liberty engines caused overheating. He immediately arranged to modify them. The *Chicago* came over the next day. Smith had arranged to have two navy motorboats race out ahead of his plane and had taxied into their wakes to get off the still, glassy surface.

The Chinese had also made social plans for the airmen though it was difficult to make time for them with the engine modification added to usual maintenance chores. Typically, "we finished our work by lantern light and then were up again before dawn," noted Nelson. But some free time was managed. The crews had learned to handle chopsticks in Japan; here, they sampled shark fins, eggs advertised as a hundred years old, and bird's nest soup—all Chinese delicacies. There was a large American colony in Shanghai, and Smith made business connections with employees of the Standard Oil Company. Its extensive facilities were made available to the airmen as the flight traveled around south Asia.

Believing their takeoff problems would continue, Smith greatly reduced the gasoline load the DWCs carried, and arranged for the next flight to be refueled by the navy off the China coast. On June 7, the first attempt to rise from the river failed. On the next try, the *Chicago* and *Boston* succeeded. The *New Orleans*, slowed in avoiding a small boat, roared on upriver, skillfully dodging thickening traffic

A Robert Sherry painting of the DWCs surrounded by sampans in the pirate harbor of Amoy

before it also rose. At midday the flight landed in rough water beside a destroyer at sea, refueled, and flew on toward Amoy. They must have felt confident, for Harding reported they dived and buzzed picturesque Chinese junks in the Formosa Strait.

They landed beside the Standard Oil pier at Amoy and slept aboard the destroyer *Preble*. Amoy was a pirate port controlled by a warlord who had defected from the Chinese Navy *with* the warship he commanded. Though the air crews did not go into town, citizens from Amoy came out aboard hundreds of sampans to see them; the crowds created the danger of damaging the seaplanes. A launch from the *Preble* charged about, barely keeping order. When departure time came, the navy could not budge the ring of boats until the launch's wake capsized several of the sampans as examples. Then the others backed off till takeoff space was cleared.

On their way to Hong Kong, the Americans got a good look at a real typhoon, luckily passing the other way. Harding saw it as "a solid mass of soot-black cloud, through which lightning flickered like a snake's tongue." The flight received a tailwind spin-off from the storm that for a while increased their speed by sixty miles per hour. Though maintenance work denied them sightseeing time, these globetrotters rated Hong Kong's harbor view the most beautiful of their journey. At this British colony, the *Chicago* was hoisted onto the Standard Oil dock and received a new pontoon, and all the DWCs had their propellers adjusted to work better in the tropic air. They took off again on the morning of June 10.

This day's destination (495 miles) was Haiphong, northern port of the French colony of Indochina (now Vietnam). Smith, the peninsula hopper, here chose to shortcut forty miles over the Luichow land neck into the Gulf of Tonkin. Roaring across at five hundred feet, Smith watched natives scatter in panic before the advance of his triangle of flying dragons. They homed in to the Standard Oil facility at the mouth of the Red River, where a French vessel was parked. There was a party all set to start on board for the Americans.

The airmen's rule of doing their airplane chores first was not understood by the French dignitaries. They boarded launches and gathered near the planes, as in Amoy. Because of language difficulties, the official greeter was sent away. By the time the Americans went on board, most of the welcomers had given up. But the French governor had waited, and so the affair was smoothed over and the fliers were entertained that evening at a grand reception ashore before again bunking with the U.S. Navy.

In the morning, three hours were spent getting off the calm lower Red River. Typical was Wade's and Ogden's *Boston,* roaring downriver at fifty-five miles per hour, swerving to avoid boats, *for twelve miles,* before the floats parted from the water. The group hoped to make it through to Saigon with a refueling halt at Tourane, but the *Chicago* had other plans. Its Liberty engine overheated, and Smith landed in a coastal lagoon, where Arnold refilled the radiator with salt water as their companions circled overhead. Takeoff was routine from a breezy sea.

But the problem was not solved; before long the *Chicago's* radiator leak became a washout, and the engine became very hot. Smith turned to the coast and into the mouth of a jungle river, getting down fast in a lagoon beside the stream. Visible motor parts glowed red and smoke streamed as the inside of the Liberty engine thrashed to pieces. The plane just missed going down in flames. Both wingmen swooped and landed beside the disabled DWC, as Arnold, out on a wing, vigorously damped down the power plant with a portable fire extinguisher.

After talking briefly, the airmen of the *Boston* and *New Orleans* turned over their water canteens and departed. In the tropic heat of late afternoon, Smith and Arnold rested in the shade of the top wing, hungry and waiting. Human reaction was slow, for the arrival of screaming sky dragons had scared off whoever lived in the jungle.

The *Chicago* was tied to a set of bamboo poles in the middle of the lagoon. The first native daring to come out was the owner of the poles, which were part of a fish trap. He pleaded with them in his language to move before they wrecked it. This was eventually understood and done. Other natives appeared, including a character in a white robe who sprinkled a few French words among his Annamese phrases. He was not interested in aiding them; he believed they had come to sell cigarettes. He would buy *if* the price was right. No deal, so he went away.

As dusk came on, three Catholic priests from a nearby mission arrived and offered to supply such food as they possessed. So Arnold went with them, but a crisis arose because they wished to be paid something. In the humble, windowless chapel where they now stood, Arnold handed them a fifty-dollar bill as the only money he carried, and declared, "Here, buy yourself windows." The eager priests then gave him, in addition to their food stock, a bottle of sacramental wine.

Arnold rejoined Smith. They spent the night slapping at mosquitos and vigilant for nosy natives who paddled near the *Chicago* to try to snip off souvenirs. The mosquitos feasted, but the pair had better luck in fending off the Annamese by firing the flare pistol and frightening them with the flashlight's beam. Martin and Harvey would have understood their lonely doubts.

CHAPTER EIGHT

Hard Traveling West

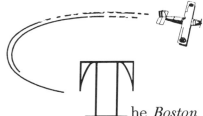

The *Boston* and *New Orleans* sped into Tourane (called Da Nang in the Vietnam War) in an hour. Nelson, as the group's engine man, got going on the problem of repairing the disabled *Chicago.* Wade would take care of hustling a U.S. destroyer down to Saigon to bring back a new Liberty. Meanwhile, Nelson would have to reach the marooned Smith and Arnold, and then figure out how to get the new engine there and installed.

Again the depth of planning by the World Flight Committee in distant Washington, D.C., paid off. Lieutenant Malcolm Lawton, advance officer for Indochina, had picked a Frenchman named Chevalier, a Standard Oil man, as the local handler in Tourane—and had chosen well. Monsieur Chevalier grasped the crisis: He looked at the map and said the fliers were down near the city of Hue, then provided an automobile and drove with Nelson three hours up the coast road. He knew the territory and was acquainted with the colonist whose property was nearest the lagoon.

Picking up food and drink for the fliers in Hue, they drove onward to this rice plantation. It was near midnight when the small expedition, recruited at the plantation, entered the totally dark, tiger-inhabited jungle, then continued their journey aboard sampans gliding through swamp waterways. Their paddlers prayed and scattered rice as peace offerings to the crocodiles of the night. Eventually their group was enlarged by the local Annamese headman and his followers, who had heard of the plane coming down. So, at three o'clock in the morning, the by-now sizeable flotilla arrived and was joyously greeted by Smith and Arnold.

The headman was openhanded. He provided three war sampans, galleys manned by ten naked rowers each; and after dawn's tropic blush, they put the *Chicago* in tow and for ten hours paddled up the jungle river to Hue, the ancient Annamese capital. Wives of the boat's crewmen scooted alongside in their smaller boats, passing over food, drink, and cigarettes. Meanwhile, in his accompanying royal galley, the headman lolled under a sunshade while being fed dainties by his favorite concubine, as his junior wives paddled the heavy galley to the rhythm of a drum. Smith and Arnold also took it easy on seat cushions under the shade of the towed plane's wing, while Nelson and Chevalier trekked back to their automobile, stopped to ready arrangements in Hue, and hurried back to Tourane.

The Mandarin's war galleys tow the *Chicago* up the jungle river, by Robert Sherry.

The new Liberty engine, U.S. Navy–delivered, was loaded into a truck, with Ogden and a party of sailors riding along, while Nelson and Chevalier led in the automobile. Ogden has remarked that he would not forget their Annamese driver, who, reckless in the darkness, four times ran the truck off the road—twice onto a cliff edge. Then the precious motor was nearly lost aboard a leaky stream ferry. But eventually, in Hue, the repair gang used the river bridge as their hoist beam, and the engine change was completed smoothly. Then the *Chicago* was able to fly on routinely into Tourane.

On June 16, the world flight trio reached Saigon; on the 18 they rounded the southern edge of Indochina and flew up to Bangkok, Siam (Thailand)—nearly six hundred miles that day. The fliers thought that Siamese hospitality was the warmest of the trip, and remembered the broiling Oriental city both from their shock at seeing dead babies drifting in the river, and the novelty of watching the royal herd of albino pink elephants.

The crews were now beginning a long westward flight route along the Asian undercontinent, and their flight commander faced an immediate choice between a thousand-mile trip around the Malay peninsula via Singapore, or a 130-mile hop over its jungle neck. Surely, engine failure over land meant a hopeless wreck below for a pontoon-geared DWC. This chance Smith had taken on before and repeated here. The Malay crossing was a hot, misty trip, with strange jungle air currents that nearly pulled them down to destruction. But they made it across and onto the Irrawaddy River at Rangoon, Burma, after a rough refueling stop in the Andaman Sea beside the U.S. destroyer *Sicard.*

Rangoon was not their happiest stopover city. Arnold toppled off a pontoon into the river, no joke when weighted in flying garb; and his rescuer Smith fell ill with dysentery (from water consumed while on the Hue lagoon). Then, at night, a large Burmese river freighter drifted straight for the three anchored DWCs. Alert U.S. naval personnel from a destroyer raced to board the vessel, knocked out the inattentive helmsman, and rolled the ship's wheel. Below, a navy launch drove in front of the freighter, absorbing the glancing crash. But the

At the typical low altitude, the *Chicago, Boston* and *New Orleans* fly across rice paddies in South Asia.

New Orleans was left with a crushed lower wing. It was June 25 before the men and planes could resume flying.

Getting off the calm, hot Irrawaddy River at Rangoon became their final wrestle with the static attraction between float surfaces and the water. The *Boston* and *New Orleans* arose, using the wake behind a departing ship, but the *Chicago* lagged. Now Wade, in the *Boston*, showed an example of why he was considered perhaps the fanciest flier in the U.S. Air Service. Returning, he held the heavy DWC to a delicate surface skim for a mile, so that the *Chicago* could rise by following the ruffled water surface.

That day they passed unseen, in the muggy monsoon atmosphere, the eastbound English world flier, MacLaren, at last under way with his second airplane. (The French and Portuguese efforts had by now failed.) Sodden Akyab, Burma, where four hundred inches of rain falls each year, was their overnight stopover. They left, in the rain, at 7 A.M. precisely, to fulfill a reckless boast by their host destroyer's skipper to the local Britons. He assured them the U.S. fliers would get off quickly, in contrast to British MacLaren's long weathered-in delay. Threading between dense monsoon downpours, they reached the Hoogli River anchorage at Calcutta, India, after a refueling landing at the Indian (now Bangladeshi) port of Chittagong.

Hard Traveling West

Calcutta, a vast city teeming with people, heat, and strange sights, enveloped the Americans. Here the DWCs were lifted from the river and carried into the spacious Maidan Park and refitted with wheels. Smith fell and broke a rib, but no delay was caused by it, though the flight commander suffered on later flights. Also, Linton Wells, the foreign correspondent who had greeted them in the Kuriles, turned up and renewed his acquaintance with the fliers.

Changing from pontoons to wheels on the *Maidan*, Calcutta, India

Linton Wells,
the newshawk hitchhiker

Wells was a globetrotter who fitted fairly well the romantic ideal of a foreign correspondent of that era. He did favors for the crew members and helped them work on their planes. As a newsman, he had a plan: He knew the DWCs would be significantly lightened by the substitution of wheels for pontoons—and he wanted to insert *his* 175 pounds onto one of the planes. What a story it would make!

After Smith's injury (he had fallen after stepping into a Calcutta sidewalk hole), Wells asked for permission to fly along. He promised to work off his passage as the needed extra hand on the ground. All three pilots turned him down, but eventually Wade agreed to carry him in the *Boston* if Smith agreed. The commander wired Washington about the matter. When no reply came by departure time, Smith allowed the reporter conditional passage.

By putting a board across the single upholstered seat in the rear cockpit of the *Boston,* both Ogden and Wells could be seated, jammed in together. This, however, caused the occupants to jut out into the slipstream. In days ahead, the planes flew through sand and dust storms which rasped the pair's exposed faces painfully. There is no public record of Ogden's complaining about his pushy fellow traveler. All the mechanicians on the world flight seemed to be very accommodating.

In leaving Calcutta, the Air Service fliers also parted from their U.S. Navy hosts, who had provided a destroyer in every port. Fortunately, for some distance their way ahead lay through overseas realms of Great Britain, with a network of Royal Air Force stations. The English, knowing of the American's favor to their national world flier, Stuart MacLaren, were helpful and efficient in hosting Smith and Company's stopovers.

Now the steamy jungles were left behind as they proceeded across inland India via Allahabad, Ambala, and Multan. Monotonous desert landscape appeared below their wings, and it got still hotter. Indeed, Multan, (now in Pakistan) was "Molten" to the locally based RAF fliers. The Americans noted that the temperature did not dip below 116 degrees while they were there. And nearby, while flying low enough to see the ground through the swirl of a dust storm they could not fly over, they reported a temperature of 156 degrees in the congested rear cockpit of the *Boston!*

Heat, grinding sand, and dust in the atmosphere forecast Liberty engine trouble. It struck the *New Orleans* outside of Multan, at a point still fifty-five miles from Karachi, India (now Pakistan). A valve ground loose and fell into a cylinder well. This caused the piston to punch holes into the crankcase. Hot oil spurted back in the crew's faces, and there was danger of the plane's catching fire. The choppy desert surface below showed no chance of surviving a forced landing.

The only favorable factor was the plane's height that day, about five thousand feet. Nelson eased back on the self-destructing engine. He successfully attempted to fly the *New Orleans* as a glider, soaring on thermal currents. There was hot air aplenty arising from the blistered land, but the heavy aircraft was no kite. So, repeatedly, Nelson gingerly gunned the engine, which rumbled and smoked and spit, but each time delivered the lift needed to soar into another slightly cooling thermal.

What was mechanician Harding doing? The Tennesseean said he was praying and singing, remembered hymns like "Jesus Savior, pilot me. . . ." In this fashion, the troubled DWC staggered, swinging and descending, all the way into Karachi. The *New Orleans* made it because this aircraft held one of the most tenacious Liberty's ever built, and it was guided by a most resourceful and cool-handed pilot.

Karachi, an oasis city in the midst of the desert near the mouth of the Indus River, had, by turn, seen all of the would-be world fliers.

All others had flown eastward; but these Americans flying westward had just about reached their halfway mark. The *Chicago, Boston,* and *New Orleans* came in on the Fourth of July, but passenger Wells had little to celebrate. Two cables had arrived for him from the United States. In one, General Patrick kicked him off the flight (after two thousand miles); and in the other, the Associated Press fired him.

The Associated Press told Wells he was fired for disobedience in not returning to his Tokyo base. Patrick felt Wells's story was too big, too exclusive, and unfairly obtained. He could foresee jealousy spoiling good relations with the rest of the media. So perhaps the Associated Press *had* been officially pressured. Anyway, the story was fudged: It was reported (and repeated in Lowell Thomas's official memorial volume) that Wells had crawled aboard the *Boston* unseen, undiscovered in the rear fuselage locker till the next stop. Then, Smith made him work off his "stowaway passage" on airplane chores as far as Karachi. Ogden must have been amused when reading about it.

Nelson had wanted to change all engines back in Calcutta, but any delay there might have allowed the oncoming monsoon season to wash out their schedule. So Fourth Division advance officer Lieutenant Harry Halvorson arranged the transfer by ship of three new Liberty engines from drippy Calcutta to arid Karachi, where there was an RAF facility that overhauled planes from the region. Two long days' work installed the new engines in the planes, so that the DWCs departed Karachi on July 7.

Now their route lay westward along coastal Persia (Iran): Chabar, Bandar Abbas, Bushire, and then inland to Baghdad, Iraq. Both flight diarists, Arnold and Harding, remarked on the awesome, desolate, saw-toothed desert over which they flew in fine weather and without a skipped engine beat. Advance Officer Halvorson had visited all these remote places, also every Indian station and emergency desert landing strip. He had contracted malaria and dysentery, and in Baghdad he learned that the last two occupants of his hotel room had both died in it of bubonic plague!

The world fliers found his arrangements up to standard, considering the places. At Bandar Abbas, for example, no fuel tanks were available, so the gasoline was stocked in two-gallon cans. Refueling

64

The crippled *New Orleans* at Karachi, India

had begun at 3:30 A.M. so the air crews could get an early start in the cooler heat of dawn. Even so, each plane was only half filled. But all area arrangements clicked, and the U.S. world flight crossed this dangerous stretch of 1,695 miles in two days.

Bandar Abbas was the principal port from which caravans of old carried the Indies wealth of silk and spice toward Europe. And beginning there, ancient history flowed beneath their wings. From Bushire, at the head of the Persian Gulf, they flew up the former Fertile Crescent, a birthplace of modern civilizations beside the Tigris and Euphrates Rivers. Flying over date palm plantations near Basra, Arnold recalled that the supposed locale of the Garden of Eden was somewhere below. Then mounds in the now-sanded-over desolation marked the memory of ancient cities. Over Babylon, the sightseer remembered that the Captive Tribes of Israel had been brought there, and it was the site of Daniel's visit to the lions' den.

65

Baghdad, renowned for past splendors in the reigns of the ca-
liphs, Moslem rulers, was now larger but still a typically hot, drab
Middle Eastern city of mud architecture. The plague was present, so
the visiting airmen didn't see, on the ground, Baghdad's great mosque
and other sights. They bunked comfortably at the large RAF station
and swapped tales with the several World War I aces there on peace-
keeping duty for the British empire.

In the morning of July 9, they set off on another desert crossing
and observed varied sand devils, minor sand-sucking whirlwinds,
twirling on the arid surface far below. Nearer to the day's destination
of Aleppo, Syria, they carefully avoided a monster sand devil that
spiraled four thousand feet high. Nelson thought "the sun shining
down on the whirling white particles gave it the appearance of a
colossal spinning top."

Syria was then a French colony, so the Americans hobnobbed
with French Air Force officers before turning in to rest a few hours
before another dawn departure. The next stop was to be Constantinople (now Istanbul), Turkey, on the edge of Europe. To get there, they
had to cross the barrier in southern Turkey of the seven- to ten-
thousand-foot-high Taurus mountains. The DWCs were no mountain
climbers; they needed to find a pass. With the help of clear weather,
they found a narrow one above the tracks of the former "Berlin to
Baghdad Railway."

The air crews paused to rest for a couple of days in Constantinople, the romantic former capital of the Turkish empire. Its harbor of
the Golden Horn, on the Sea of Marmara at the south end of the
Bosporus Strait, had been a funnel of commerce since ancient times.
The exhausted airmen were well looked after by Halvorson and the
European area advance officer, Major Carlyle Wash. Flight Commander Smith, his rib still a painful bother, looked as wan as poor,
ailing Halvorson. For them all, it had been seventy-nine hundred
miles of hard traveling west from Hong Kong. But now they were
slightly ahead of schedule and had landed in Europe (with Asia still
in view across the strait), and felt greatly encouraged by having come
this far safely.

CHAPTER NINE

S O S the *Boston!*

Outfitted with pages of detailed European flight plans prepared by Major Wash in his continental travels, the homeward-bound Magellans of the air departed from Constantinople on the morning of July 12. Bucharest, Romania, was aerial port of call for this day, a mere 350 miles distant. When they landed there, absolutely no one was on hand to greet them because of a communications foul-up. What luck! was the reaction of the fliers, for they knew that their greatest "ordeals by banquet" lay along the European route. A bit later, though, they were sorry to decline an invitation from the Queen of Romania (and her daughters) to join them at their summer palace.

Next morning, the trio took off for Belgrade, Yugoslavia, following the Danube River upstream through its "Iron Gate" notch in the Transylvanian Alps. Since they were pushed by a tailwind, Smith signaled to bypass Belgrade and continue into Budapest, Hungary. The U.S. diplomats below were left with the unpleasant duty of explaining this to their snubbed Yugoslav hosts. Following lunch in Hungary, they hopped on over to Vienna, Austria, for the night.

Though they had enjoyed, in turn, the different ways and wonders of Oriental and Moslem cultures, the Americans were now pleased to find the more familiar comforts of cosmopolitan Europe.

Arnold noted that the suite he shared with Smith in Vienna's Imperial Hotel had rooms "about the size of the ballroom in an American hotel," and "we had twin beds, each on a raised dais, draped with silk canopies," with mattresses "so soft we sank right down almost out of sight."

It would have been great to sleep past noon, but as usual they hustled out early in the morning to fly on west, still for a distance tracking up the Danube valley toward the mighty river's source in Germany's Black Forest. This was July 14, France's national holiday, Bastille Day, marking the beginning of the French Revolution, and the Americans vowed to get there. After refueling at Strasbourg, across the Rhine River in eastern France, the world flight detoured northward to view the former battlefields of World War I's battered Western Front. Wade, Arnold, and Smith had flown over them earlier at the war's end.

Then they turned west toward Paris and were met by a swarm of welcoming French Air Force planes that led them across the central part of the city. There the fliers respectfully circled above the Arch of Triumph, where an eternal flame burned for World War I's Unknown Soldier. Then they settled into Le Bourget airfield. There, thousands of onlookers surged dangerously close to the three DWCs, and the pilots revved their motors and taxied into a hangar to avoid them.

Immediately, the world fliers were swept up by "more generals, ambassadors, cabinet ministers and celebrities than we had encountered in all the rest of our lives," in Wade's phrase. Even here, in the official glitter, their flight discipline survived, for as soon as they could, the air crews turned back and performed their maintenance chores before leaving for the city. (The French quipped they were "feeding their horses.")

In the evening, they viewed the naughty but nice dance revue of the famed Folies Bergère. All six "red-blooded American heroes" fell asleep! Prodded awake by an amazed Frenchman, Wade murmured, "Huh!" in appreciation of the prancing line of scantily clad dancers—and nodded right off again.

Paris: *Vive les aviateurs Americains!*

It was understandable: They had left distant Constantinople only two days before, had flown ten hours on this Bastille Day, and had, in previous days, roared ten thousand punishing miles across hot Asia. So they slept! Their hand-printed proclamations posted on their Paris hotel doors warned all away till 9 A.M., except for fire "AND NOT EVEN THEN UNLESS THE FIREMEN HAVE GIVEN UP HOPE!"

The lieutenants spent the next day in the company of the President of France and top-ranked American General Pershing, who was visiting Paris. Wade and Arnold, who knew Paris, happily managed to escort their companions to a few of their wartime hangouts in the precious scraps of time between affairs of state.

When, on the following morning of July 16, the world flight departed for London, Smith and Company, for easy navigation, followed a marvel in the sky—an airliner. Since the war, a network of commercial airlines linked European capitals with passenger services. It was

69

Wade and Nelson gleefully tour Paris.

a surprise to these far-flown airmen to see the busy traffic of modern, enclosed airliners flying in and out of Paris's Le Bourget Airfield. It would be several years before airlines appeared in the United States. On this occasion, their guiding British airliner reduced speed so that the DWCs could keep pace with it.

Typically, the aviator on the ground becomes the critic of his airborne brethren, and so it was at Croydon Airfield, London. The grassy earth of the runway bulged a little across its middle, and local pilots watched as strangers landing there usually bounced ungracefully. But Smith, leading in the *Chicago,* handled the unevenness well, coasting in soft and smooth, as did the following DWCs. To these veteran fliers, Croyden's surface was pool table velvet compared with some of the places they'd dropped into during the 17,450 miles they had flown to date.

Next, the onlookers' attention focused on the *New Orleans* after it had taxied up and switched off. The first thing Harding did while still in the cockpit was to light up a cigarette. Nearby, cautious Britons gasped and cringed, half-expecting an explosion. Then Nelson climbed down and doffed his aviator's helmet in smiling greeting. Why, the man was bald! Someone said it out loud, "What on earth is that old cove doing flying round the world? He ought to be nursing his grandchildren by the fireside instead of cavorting around in an aeroplane."

Well, so much for first impressions! The English were edgy because their world flier, A. Stuart MacLaren, was missing in the bleak Kuriles. (He turned up safe.) Mrs. MacLaren gamely was on hand to thank Smith for arranging the shipment of the second plane to her husband, when he was stranded at Akyab, Burma. These Kuriles veterans assured her that communications in the stormy North Pacific were certainly spotty, and to keep faith.

The Americans attended the customary welcoming banquet that evening, and in the morning flew to the north of England, landing at the airfield of the Blackburn Aeroplane Company at Brough, beside the Humber River. There the engines would be replaced and the planes completely overhauled including replacing floats again for the last ocean hop. Some of the fliers took time out from these vital

The *Chicago* rests at London.

Hank Ogden does aircraft maintenance in England.

preparations to attend functions in London. However, an invitation from the King of England came late in their stay and had to be declined.

The world flight had not been delayed by weather since India, but now faced fog and storm across the North Atlantic. No airplane had yet flown this ocean from east to west, so all those involved with the U.S. attempt at closing the global circle vowed that they would not fail this final major challenge. General Patrick ordered a pause at Brough from July 17 until month's end. August offered the best weather for their routing via Iceland, Greenland, and Labrador; and it allowed the U.S. Navy to place ships in position to protect the flight.

The DWC overhaul at Brough went forward despite a serious accident. One day, the chain suspending the *Chicago* snapped during working hours and the plane crashed down several feet, demolishing its new pontoons. Luckily, no one was beneath it. Also fortunately, the World Flight Committee had laid in complete stock here for the planned four-plane fleet. So the *Seattle's* pontoons were left over to be fitted on the *Chicago.*

On July 30, after a lengthy run along the calm Humber River, the *Chicago, Boston,* and *New Orleans* arose and, in so-so weather, flew north along the Scottish coast to Kirkwall harbor in the Orkney Islands group beyond the British mainland. Smith conferred with Admiral Magruder aboard the U.S. cruiser *Richmond* about the forthcoming ocean crossing. The world flight had been clipping along of late, and hopes were high. Smith and Company had overcome the miseries of the Aleutian/Kuriles area. What could be worse? Crossing the far north Atlantic! It would take all thirty-one days of August to complete this dangerous and stubborn portion of the route.

Arnold and Smith sightsee in Kirkwall, Orkney Islands.

By August, the U.S. Navy was on station with the cruisers *Richmond* and *Raleigh,* and the destroyers *Billingsley, Reid,* and *Barry,* in a protective arc along the 555 miles of foggy ocean between Scotland and Iceland. On August 2 there was radio consensus among them that the North Atlantic weather was passable all the way. The world flight responded, climbing out of Kirkwall into a sky and seascape gray in tone above and below. They had flown in their usual tight triangle formation about twenty-five miles when the trio entered a dense wall of fog.

Here there recurred the problem the fliers experienced in Alaskan fogs: Despite their closeness, the aircraft crews could no longer see one another. They drifted, and then the *New Orleans* was abruptly upset by a propeller blast from one of the other DWCs and fell unseen into a spinning dive. There was no point of reference in the sightless gray wool fog that the pilot could use to try to recover. The unflappable veteran Nelson locked his eye upon his instruments, relying on what they told him about speed and direction. Gradually he guided the fuel-heavy *New Orleans* out of the spin, barely pulling out above the tossing, grasping sea beneath the fog.

Meanwhile, the *Chicago* and *Boston* climbed into a clear level between the fog and a higher cloud strata. They circled for a half hour, waiting, then descended to seek their absent wingman. Worried, Smith signaled a turn back. En route, they looked for, but could not find, the *Richmond* in the soup below, and so they dropped their urgent message into the main street of Kirkwall, before returning to the harbor to await word on the fate of the *New Orleans.*

Nelson navigated northwestward through the thin, clear level between fog and ocean. After the fog faded, he climbed high through cloud layers. After a look around for the others, he guided the *New Orleans* on course toward Iceland. He and Harding were reassured to see the jagged peaks of the Faeroe Islands probing through the lower clouds where they were supposed to be. They continued toward Iceland, encouraged despite an engine running rough because of a problem with the oil circulation.

Abruptly, both fog and clouds ended, and the men of the *New Orleans* saw below them the rising smoke from the stacks of the destroyer *Billingsley.* Swooping, they messaged, asking if the others had passed and received by whistle blast a negative reply. Nearer Iceland the weather again worsened, and they did not see the *Raleigh* below. But the mountainous, glacier-seamed bulk of Iceland could not be hidden. The *New Orleans* landed at the fishing village of Hornafjord at 5:37 P.M.; the first airplane ever to fly to Iceland—and piloted by a descendant of the Vikings, as were the Icelanders.

Relieved by news of their comrades' success, Smith and Arnold, Wade and Ogden set off on the morning of August 3 for Hornafjord in weather similar to that of the day before. Just before 11:00 A.M., flying at five hundred feet and about 150 miles out, the *Boston* was seen to veer to the right in a shallow dive, ending in Wade's expert emergency landing on the crest of a swell in the rough sea. Wade signaled that the *Boston*'s oil system had failed, as could be seen by the broad smear of oil running from the engine cover. He and Ogden, and the precious *Boston* as well, would have to be rescued.

Smith and Arnold's DWC soon roared across the wireless station in the Faeroe Islands, and dropped a vital message. Then Smith guided the *Chicago* out to the *Billingsley,* miles seaward to the northwest. Arnold's tossed message missed the swiftly moving destroyer. Now he tied his last scribbled note to his life preserver and hurled the lot. It, too, narrowly missed the deck, but a sailor of the *Billingsley,* an unsung hero, dived into the icy ocean and retrieved it. Thereafter, three blasts of the destroyer's whistle signaled its turn to race toward the marked position of the *Boston.* The *Richmond,* to the south of the marooned fliers, also put on steam to reach the locale after getting radio notification. The *Chicago* reluctantly flew on alone through gloom of foggy rain to land safely at Hornafjord.

The "cradle of the deep" now rocked the *Boston* in dangerous twenty-foot swings, with the sea becoming slowly choppier in lowering visibility. A lone sea gull joined Wade and Ogden for a while. About 2:00 P.M., a ship came into view, but passed on without seeing the pair's waving or their fired rocket signals. Ogden pulled out a map, and together they guessed, in black humor, how long it would take the *Boston* to drift to Norwegian shores. Then, at 3:30 P.M., a fishing trawler appeared on the horizon, and it seemed on course in their

Above: Moments before the botched attempt to hoist the *Boston* aboard the USS *Richmond*. Below: The end of the *Boston*

direction! As it neared, Wade pinged rifle shots into its bow—to be sure to arouse its crew's attention. Soon a voice hallooed in needlessly proper English fashion, "Do you want any help?"

After much maneuvering to no result—including a moment when the *Boston* was lifted by the waves and nearly crashed onto the small vessel's deck—a line between was secured. But it was no-go for a tow, with the ship and the windblown plane bent on contrary directions. At this point the *Billingsley* arrived, and right afterward, the *Richmond*. Because the sea was worsening in violence, the *Richmond*'s skipper, Captain Lyman Cotten, decided to attempt hoisting the plane aboard. It was lightened of equipment and the gasoline drained away. Wade and Ogden boarded the cruiser, too.

But the DWC was heavier than the cruiser's own scout plane, and at the critical point the lurching burden caused the hoist beam to collapse. The *Boston* dropped back, and the force of the impact badly damaged the seaplane. Dismayed, Wade quickly estimated it would require new wings and pontoons, as well as another engine and propeller, to fly again.

Still, he and Ogden wouldn't give up. They proposed that the aircraft be taken apart on the sea and brought aboard in pieces. A few very brave *Richmond* crewmen tried to do that and were nearly swept away to their deaths. All the *Richmond* could do was to slowly tow the wreck toward the Faeroe Islands, seventy miles away, and through that night it did so.

But at 5:00 A.M., with a rocky, mournful Faeroe shore in sight, the derelict *Boston* capsized and the sea entered its empty tanks. It was a desolate end, with sorrowing Wade and Ogden looking on helplessly. After the *Richmond* had delivered the hapless fliers to Iceland, Wade, meeting Smith, was overcome by emotion. The two veteran fliers hugged silently.

CHAPTER TEN

By Greenland's
Icy Mountains

On August 5 the remaining world fliers, Smith and Arnold, Nelson and Harding, flew the *Chicago* and the *New Orleans* two hundred ninety miles along Iceland's southern coast in blustery weather, and neatly landed amid a forest of masts in the harbor of the Icelandic capital of Reykjavik. Here the Americans learned that their English rival MacLaren's world flight attempt had ended in the ocean on the other side of their harsh arctic world. His second plane had been damaged beyond repair in a landing on the foggy, stormy waters of the Bering Sea, off those same Kommandorski Islands that the U.S. planes had previously visited illegally in an emergency.

Now the U.S. fliers had to wait in Reykjavik for over two weeks. Iceland, though no Riviera, was far from totally ice-covered. Its winters were long in darkness; but the warmth of the Gulf Stream flowing up from the tropics washed its southern shores and made the coasts habitable. Over one hundred and fifty thousand people made a living from farming and fishing. The Viking-descended Icelanders were friendly to these airborne adventurers. Nelson had come "home" in culture and language; but Harding remarked he'd rather have been stranded in Paris.

The fliers' stranding occurred because the next big arctic island, Greenland, remained remote and unapproachable. Ice was the principal feature of this misnamed land mass—about 98 percent of the surface of the huge island is ice. The division advance officer, Lieutenant LeClaire Schulze, had properly waited for the height of summer to go into its forbidding eastern coast. However, with the world flight coming on, he remained locked in pack ice aboard a cooperating Danish ship forty miles away from delivering the stock of fuel and parts to the next planned stop, Angmagssalik, Greenland.

Finally, Schulze was able to get into Angmagssalik, but lingering ice in its harbor made the site unusable. The hardworking officer found an alternate sheltered strip of water on that bleak coast, but then a series of storms and further ice movements prevented him from stocking the place. The news correspondents gathered in Reykjavik believed that the world flight would be cancelled right here.

This was selling the grit and ingenuity of Smith, Patrick, and their associates too short. Lieutenant Bissell, the resourceful Alaskan advance officer, was now serving on the other, western side of Greenland. He selected and recommended the open fjord at Fredericksdal, on west Greenland's southern cape, as a replacement for icebound Angmagssalik, and his choice was accepted by Smith and Patrick. But the new haven was three hundred miles further along, adding a familiar problem.

With nonstop distance now stretched to 830 miles, the gasoline load was a heavy factor. Neither plane could take off when it tried on August 18. A second attempt, with the DWCs wallowing through sea swells, caused damage to the *Chicago's* pontoons and snapped the propeller of the *New Orleans.* While repairs went on, a likable Italian airman, Antonio Locatelli, who had arrived with his crew in a big, new amphibious aircraft, received permission to accompany the Americans and share their unique on-seas naval protection. Locatelli was practicing a far north Atlantic crossing before attempting a flight across the North Pole.

On August 21, Smith, Nelson, and Locatelli all got off from Reykjavik. The new Italian plane could not fly as slowly as the DWCs and

The *New Orleans* in the harbor of Reykjavík, Iceland

soon pulled ahead into a clear western horizon. The world flight pair roared by the cruiser *Richmond,* impressing its skipper with their boldness:

> . . . It was truly a flight to test the skill and courage of the hardiest aviator. As they swept by the *Richmond* close enough to the bridge for every feature of the aviators to be recognized, it made a lump come up in one's throat to realize how fragile were these man-made ships of the air and how many hundreds of miles of ice and fog and restless waters lay ahead of them ere they reached their next haven in the bleak fjord with its towering walls that is Fredericksdal.

Beyond the day's halfway point, the fliers passed over the destroyer *Barry*—and its signal flags told them that the weather had really worsened ahead. But they, for reasons of fuel and temperament, would continue to Greenland—or destruction!

Then, some distance beyond the *Barry,* the crew of the *Chicago,* with the *New Orleans* trailing closely on its left, saw before them a towering curtain of thick, bluish fog. Its base lay near the ocean while its top level was unknown. Smith judged its height to be well above the eight-thousand-foot flight ceiling that the DWCs could manage that day. So the two planes descended to enter the mist belt at bottom. Skimming just above the white caps at first, they found visibility, hampered by fog patches, sometimes lowering to thirty feet above the waves. This was "on the deck" flying as it had been in Alaskan days. When they had flown to about seventy-five miles off the Greenland coast, they began to glimpse an added distraction: assorted white objects, then masses of them in the sea—icebergs!

Snow falls on Greenland and does not melt. Layers accumulate, and their weight squeezes the snow into glacier ice which flows over centuries toward the island's sea edges. Pushed off the end of land, the glacial masses "calve," cracking off in thunderous crashes into the ocean. Greenland is the busiest iceberg manufacturer of the earth's northern hemisphere. And though nine-tenths of its bulk floats submerged, the iceberg may still rear fantastic peaks far above the waves.

For the air crews, here began hours of life-or-death intensity— peering forward with aching eyes to penetrate foggy gloom that might abruptly reveal a gleaming white ice mountain immediately ahead, then needing instant reflexes to control stick and rudder pedals. "We were traveling along at a speed of ninety miles per hour," recalled Smith, "and could see only between a hundred and a hundred fifty feet ahead, so use your own imagination as to how soon a plane traveling at that speed could use up the distance that we could see, and then try and figure out how little time was left us to sight a berg ahead, decide which way to turn, and then execute the maneuver." And the closer they approached Greenland, the thicker was the iceberg population on the sea.

Dodging to either side was best, but occasionally, when confronted by a larger berg, it was necessary to haul back on the stick wheel and zoom up and over. Climbing into blank fog was followed by a dangerous descent to again sight along the sea surface.

As they reckoned to be nearing land, with hopes the fog would lift there, Smith, with Nelson tight behind and left, came out of a heavy band of soup and saw immediately before him a monstrous ice wall. In that second Smith decided this iceberg was too tall to get over, and so slammed the *Chicago* hard right as Nelson peeled off the *New Orleans* left and vanished. The maneuver was so close that the airmen in the *Chicago* believed that both left wing tips may have brushed the berg's edge as the DWC skidded past.

No time for relief or letdown, or wondering about their wingman's fate—more bergs appeared and were dodged, and finally a darker mass loomed as the high sea cliffs of Greenland. Smith gratefully turned the *Chicago* southward here, but the fog did not relent. ". . . We would dodge a white shadow, and then a black one would suddenly loom up on the opposite side. Once in a while, when concentrating all our attention on a particularly ominous-looking patch of cliff to our right, we would instinctively feel something sliding by the wing on our left. Turning quickly we would be just in time to see a ghostlike berg that we had missed by only ten feet or so, melting into the gloom. Perhaps it was a sudden icy draft from the berg, like the cold hand of death, that would cause us to turn our heads."

This blind flying continued until the *Chicago* turned westward after passing Cape Farewell at Greenland's southern tip. Abruptly the

The *Chicago* and *New Orleans* pictured at the moment the iceberg appears through the mist, by Robert Sherry

fog ended. Happy and relieved, they flew on in clear skies, turning now northwest along the mountainous coast. Ahead soon appeared another fog mass lying even tighter on the water. But Smith was able to gun the DWC to climb over the soup. He continued in the clear using the peaks emerging from the fog to navigate to where he believed Fredericksdal fjord lay beneath the clouds. The *New Orleans* was not seen.

Smith and Arnold circled, peering down to look for a break in the clouds. Then, Smith wrote, "the All-Wise Providence, who had already spared our lives a dozen times on this day's journey, parted the clouds for us so that there was a shaft of light extending down to the sea." And at the base of the providential shaft was a ship! The *Chicago* spiraled down, and Smith gratefully landed beside the Danish cutter *Island Falk,* on station for them, and then taxied several miles into the calmer depths of the fjord, a deep mountainous inlet. It was 5:30 P.M. What a ten-hour day they had had flying from Reykjavik!

By Greenland's Icy Mountains

The gaunt, towering sides of their harbor inspired awe, but Smith's and Arnold's silence as they performed routine chores was mainly because of their fears for the *New Orleans* crew. It seemed unlikely that two miracles could occur at that awful iceberg. Yet, forty minutes later, the world fliers below rejoiced at the sound of a Liberty engine above, approaching from the south and then circling unseen overhead.

Nelson, after escaping the berg, had continued south. Not wanting to meet the thickening ice near the coast, he had made a wide turn around Greenland until he came into the area of clearing. He and Harding looked about for the *Chicago* as they came on northwest along the route of visible peaks, and, failing to see their flight leader, they, too, feared and guessed the worst for their fellows. The cloud shaft remained open for the *New Orleans'* descent into Fredericksdal Fjord; and they were delighted to see the *Chicago* at anchor there. After sending a radio message to the U.S. fleet commander of their safe arrival, minus Locatelli, the reunited Americans had, according to Arnold, the most joyous party Greenland ever would host.

What had happened to the Italian plane? When Locatelli entered the belt of fog and began meeting icebergs, he turned and flew back a bit, preparing to set down on the ocean in his big flying boat and await clearing conditions. But, like MacLaren, he misjudged the rough sea in landing. The Locatelli plane, though it floated, was too damaged to fly again. Several U.S. Navy ships launched a systematic search, but they were hampered by the persisting poor weather. On the fourth night, a lookout on the *Richmond* glimpsed a distant flare fired by the bedraggled castaways, and Locatelli and his crew were rescued.

Danish Greenland had a native population of less than forty thousand Eskimos tucked away here and there in fjord villages, as at Fredericksdal. This group hunted and fished mainly by traditional means, and the far-traveled Americans admired their skill in handling the light, skin-covered "kayak" boats. Tied in water-tight, the Eskimo could roll his kayak like a stunt plane. Another spectator sport enjoyed by the fliers was worry-free iceberg-watching. A glacier front was not far away and a parade of mostly small bergs floated past the village. Nelson tells of one large iceberg that tipped over as they looked on and was a good five minutes in bobbing and splashing before achieving balance again.

One night, small pieces of floating ice punched holes in the *Chicago's* floats, and Smith went into the frigid water, as he had done in Alaska, to pump the pontoons dry and patch them. On August 24, under the usual fog and gloom of this fjord, the *Chicago* and *New Orleans* fishtailed through the morning's icebergs and got off for the 150-mile flight on up Greenland's coast to Ivigtut, chosen as the area's main world flight supply base. On the way, both planes were tossed about by side blasts of wind as they rounded fjord headlands—williwaws off Greenland's icy mountains. The weather was fine at their

The *Chicago* and *New Orleans* sheltering at Ivigtut, Greenland

We're all together ready for the North Atlantic. Left to right are Wade, Nelson, Arnold, Ogden, Smith, and Harding.

destination, where the U.S. cruiser *Milwaukee* lay below; and they would be reunited with passenger Lieutenant Bissell, their Alaskan mentor.

Bissell had succeeded in laying ramps on the bleak Ivigtut beach, so the DWCs could be pulled ashore for maintenance. Both engines were pulled and replaced in preparation for the expedition's last ocean hop. North America was the prize, beckoning from 560 miles across the Davis Strait. If they succeeded, they would be the first airmen to have flown the North Atlantic, as well the Pacific, westbound in an airplane.

CHAPTER ELEVEN

To Icy Tickle
and Triumph

he next port of call across the frigid
Davis Strait was Icy Tickle, an aptly named place at the edge of
Labrador's barren rock mass. A radio report of expected fair weather
there crackled across to Ivigtut on the evening of August 30. The U.S.
air crews responded at 8:25 A.M., August 31, flying out through another
dangerous mixture of fog and icebergs, then climbing safely as the
weather improved on their southwestern course. However, mechanical woes appeared aboard the *Chicago.* Wingman Nelson signaled
Smith of a significant oil smear oozing from the commander's new
Liberty engine. Then, two hundred miles short of Labrador, both
motor- and wind-driven fuel pumps failed in the *Chicago.*

This was grave, though not immediately fatal. The failure cut off
the main gasoline tanks, leaving a gravity-feed reserve from a lesser
tank in the top wing. Its supply was too small to carry them across; but
the manufacturer, Douglas, had supplied a hand pump that could be
used to boost gasoline from the lower tanks into the upper gravity-
feed reserve.

When, back in Seattle, Smith was seeking his new mechanician,
he asked Arnold, "Will you work like the devil?" And Arnold eagerly
replied, "Sure, I'll work like a whole flock of devils!" Now the mechanician stripped to the waist and went to work pumping endlessly.

Ivigtut, Greenland: The takeoff for Icy Tickle

Certainly, as time passed, he became tired, sore, in pain—but he persevered. Arnold was a young man in prime physical condition; and he also had the incentive to go on whenever he glanced over the side at the wind-whipped, icy sea and imagined how short a swim it would be! After an hour his right arm became numb, but Arnold somehow continued pumping.

In the *Chicago*'s front cockpit, Smith, after tens of thousands of air miles' partnership, had complete confidence in Arnold's ability. But there were other worrisome factors: The continuing oil leak must at some time burn out the engine. Would they still be out over the strait? The ocean today looked impossible as a resting place. The North Atlantic was now throwing a forty-mile-per-hour headwind to delay them.

Arnold worked the hand pump for nearly three hours, and the large supply of oil originally put in the new Liberty engine lasted. At 3:20 P.M., the *Chicago* and the *New Orleans* slipped down onto the bay at Icy Tickle, completing the historic ocean crossing. They stepped ashore on a flat Labrador rock and were congratulated by Admiral Magruder of the navy. Arnold shook with his left hand, for it would be many hours before his dangling right arm became usable again.

Following a day of repairs on the *Chicago,* the two planes turned southward along Canada's coast. The world flight was now turning into a triumphal procession. Congratulatory messages were flowing in from the powerful and famous, topped by President Coolidge and Secretary of War Weeks.

Of more ordinary note, they flew across a headland on which sprouted woody vegetation—the first trees they had seen since Britain. The veteran pairs skimmed under a belt of fog lying on Belle Isle

Arriving in North America via a flat rock at Icy Tickle, Labrador

Strait and dodged the black shadow of a ship. As they coasted over the rocky fangs of northeast Newfoundland, the airmen saw many shipwrecks. They landed soon after in Hawke's Bay, there spending a final night aboard a U.S. destroyer.

In the morning, September 3, the *Chicago* and the *New Orleans* continued 430 miles southwest, first along Newfoundland's inner western coast, then hopping Cabot Strait in fair weather to the Canadian province of Nova Scotia. A Royal Canadian Air Force plane escorted them to the day's destination of Pictou Bay. They joyfully spotted another DWC riding at anchor in the harbor, for General Patrick had ordered the original training DWC equipped and ferried up to Canada as the *Boston II.* Wade and Ogden were at dockside for a welcome reunion.

The Nova Scotians staged a parade with bagpipes as the fliers waited a day because of weather ahead. The *Chicago, Boston II,* and *New Orleans* departed for Boston on September 5, but the planes met a vast area of dense fog along the Maine coast, and Smith signaled a precautionary landing in a cove at Mere Point in Casco Bay. So the world flight returned to American soil after being abroad since April 6. The summer people still lingering in this resort area put on a fish dinner and provided accommodations for their unexpected but highly welcome guests. In the morning, as the crews awaited gasoline, the sky reverbrated with the drone of ten Liberty engines. General Patrick and most of the World Flight Committee had flown up to escort the world fliers onto Boston Harbor.

Though thousands of Bostonians and a full crop of VIPs waited on the dockside area, Smith and Company stayed to perform their usual postflight chores before going ashore, where the flight commander received Patrick's fervent handshake. The general had risked the Air Service's reputation as well as his own on the great circle venture. He had endured the helplessness of a distant commander dependent on eight, then six, then four line officers. Smith, faced with the new technology of a nationwide radio hookup, said simply, "Hello, folks, I'm glad to be home." The fliers were presented with gifts and at their hotel they each found a dress uniform for their very social evening.

The *Chicago, Boston II* and *New Orleans,* with a flying escort, pass over the Statue of Liberty, by Robert Sherry.

In the morning, though, it was back to the planes, where the switch to wheels was completed that day. On September 8 they flew with a sizable escort to New York's Mitchell Field. A vast crowd there broke through the police lines to try to snatch bits of the plane for souvenirs. More celebrities greeted them; but the air crews stayed out of Manhattan and left early in the morning for Washington, D.C.

The weather became cloudy, with a stiff headwind that forced a refueling stop at Aberdeen, Maryland. Then the *New Orleans'* engine abruptly quit (broken timing gear), and Nelson landed in a large Maryland pasture. Patrick was still escorting, and with a couple of wingmen swooped down and landed alongside. The general directed Nelson to continue on to Washington in one of his planes. Harding was left to oversee the *New Orleans.* Because of these delays, President Coolidge waited three hours at rainy Washington for the world fliers. It is recorded he did so without audible complaint.

Air Service General Billy Mitchell accompanied the six aerial Magellans while they were in Washington; and it was at his suggestion

92

that a young journalist, Lowell Thomas, was signed on to be the world flight historian and publicist. Thomas, beginning a half century as the foremost American commentator on adventure, wrote a book, *The First World Flight,* tracing the six-month flight in the airmen's own words. This record is especially valuable because not one of the fliers afterward published a book-length memoir.

As for the upcoming transcontinental portion, Thomas wrote

> They . . . still had three thousand miles to go in airplanes that in spite of their sturdiness had long since passed their allotted span. Constant attention to business was therefore necessary by day; while by night they had no rest, for at each and every stop between Boston and Seattle they met old friends and new ones, responded to toasts, gave interviews, were the center of civic functions, and lived a life which is known to be perilous to nerves and digestion.

It was the principal duty of their last division advance officer, Lieutenant Burdette Wright, to schedule (or fend off) the many social requests stretching all the way to Seattle.

President Coolidge, here posed with Smith and Secretary of War Weeks, waited three hours in rainy Washington, D.C., to greet the American world flight heroes.

On September 13, the world flight trio flew on to Dayton, Ohio. They penetrated the foul weather lying over Pennsylvania's Allegheny Mountains, a graveyard of early aviation. Their escort planes turned back, but Smith continued, though unacquainted with the rugged terrain. He took them through in single file above the utility poles along a railway—"iron track navigation"—and luckily no tunnels! McCook Field, Dayton, was the research and development base of the Air Service, and "home" to the varied specialists of the world flight who found many friends waiting for them.

The *Chicago, Boston II,* and *New Orleans* were checked for physical fitness, as were their crews, and passed to continue via a looping route of Chicago, Illinois; Omaha, Nebraska; St. Joseph, Missouri; Muskogee, Oklahoma; Dallas, Sweetwater, and El Paso, Texas; Tucson, Arizona; and San Diego, California. This southern crossing of the west was chosen to avoid the Rockies, for the DWCs never appreciated mountains.

San Diego was a contender as their true city of origin, for at the Air Service base of Rockwell Field, the DWCs had begun their continuous north-by-northwest course. Here, a final engine change was finished overnight by the Air Service mechanics while the air crews performed socially. On September 23 there was the short hop to the DWCs' hometown of Santa Monica. Up to a quarter-million southern Californians watched the trio land at Clover Field on an acre of rose

Almost home: The *Chicago* crosses San Diego, California.

Back at Seattle, it's all over but the reminiscing (Martin, Nelson, Arnold, Wade, Smith, Ogden).

petals. Then came the charge of the souvenir seekers. The planes were shielded, but, according to Smith:

> Burly policemen helped us on our way. People were tearing bits off clothes and snipping off buttons. . . . One lady cut a chunk out of my collar with a penknife. And another got hold of my ear—I suppose by mistake. Somebody else took a keepsake out of the seat of my trousers. . . .

The fliers were some time in wading through the crowds to greet Donald Douglas and thank him for building their wonderfully rugged DWCs.

Crowd security was much better at San Francisco, and flying on up to Seattle via Eugene, Oregon, and Vancouver, Washington, was routine. And so on September 28, 1924, in pretty good weather, the veteran world flight approached Sand Point Airfield at Seattle. Before landing, they emerged from their customary triangle formation to fly low and all abreast to symbolize their sharing of the record. The aerial global circle was closed at 1:28 P.M. after 26,345 miles flown (much of it at five hundred feet or below) in 363 hours and 7 minutes of air time. The new Magellans had been tired for a long time, even as their pride grew. They had outlasted many different kinds of hostile elements and mechanical failures to open the door to worldwide aviation.

CHAPTER TWELVE

Final Verses

ublic attention to the world fliers waned within months. The big publicity boost the U.S. Air Service had sought, and Smith and Company had so handsomely delivered, was dissipated in the following year by the hue and cry of General Billy Mitchell's court-martial. Perhaps it was hard to hold a nation's imagination with "a committee led by a Smith." The public switched its attention to who would first fly the Atlantic solo and found, in 1927, their perfect air hero in "the lone eagle," Charles A. Lindbergh.

The world flight record was accepted as a worthy stunt that would in the future become routine with the establishment of world-wide aviation facilities. It showed, as well, the feasibility of global aerial military operations. But in 1924 it was believed that long-range air passenger travel of the future would certainly occur aboard dirigibles—and in 1929 Germany's *Graf Zeppelin* did carry twenty passengers around the world in twenty-one days amid comforts equal to those of first-class ocean liner passage.

World flight received its first individual hero in Wiley Post, who in 1931 flew around the world in eight days with Harold Gatty as navigator; then, in 1933, Post repeated the feat alone in his Lockheed Vega *Winnie Mae,* shaving a day off his previous record. There were many other world fliers—a deluge after World War II. Stunts included a helicopter flight around the world, a light plane circle over both poles, and the nonrefueled, nonstop flight of Dick Rutan and Jeana Yeager in *Voyager* in 1986.

Dependable transoceanic passenger transportation in flying boats appeared in the 1930s; a land-based around-the-world commercial air schedule was established in 1947 by Pan American World Airways, using Lockheed Constellation airliners. The jumbo-jet age cut all passenger flying time by half. Today you can, for a few thousand dollars, fly around the world in a weekend. Using Seattle as the historic place of departure, leave at 1:05 P.M. Friday and return at 11:35 A.M. Sunday (by current schedules).

What of the bold airmen of the first world flight? Patrick had Smith's chances for promotion jumped a thousand places ahead of fellow officers; Nelson and Wade were advanced five hundred places. But the promotions didn't come for Nelson and Wade, and by 1928, they and all of the mechanics had left the Army Air Corps, as it was then called, drawn by opportunities in civilian aviation.

Captain Lowell Smith stayed on, pioneering in the 1930s' planning for use of of gliders to deliver troops. But he did not progress rapidly in command; perhaps his silent nature held him back. At the end of World War II, when he was killed in a fall from a horse, he was a colonel commanding an Arizona training base for bomber crews.

Leslie Arnold, Smith's personable companion onboard the *Chicago,* went with the early airlines—first with a predecessor of TWA, later at Eastern Airlines as a vice president. In World War II, he reentered the AAF serving in England, and came out a major general.

Leigh Wade, of the *Boston(s),* became an airplane salesman with Latin America as his territory. In World War II, he reentered the AAF and commanded all air activity around Cuba. Later, he was sent as air attaché (military diplomat) to Greece and Brazil. He became a major general.

Hank Ogden, Wade's associate, held a series of civilian aviation jobs till joining the Lockheed Aircraft Corporation. In World War II, he supervised all Lockheed activities in England and became a Lockheed vice president.

Erik Nelson of the *New Orleans* went to Boeing Aircraft Corporation as sales manager. He was also active in the creation of United Airlines. Back in the AAF in World War II, he worked on the engineering aspects of the B-29 bomber program and became a brigadier general. In postwar years he was a consultant to SAS (Scandinavian Airlines) on its transoceanic routes.

Tennesseean Jack Harding, who rode the backseat of the *New Orleans,* was a founder of Florida Airways, which was absorbed into Eastern Airlines. He, too, worked with Boeing for a while. The savvy mechanician later became a successful manufacturer of his own fuel valve, which was widely used on American bombers and military transport planes.

What of the aircraft? The *Seattle* was pulled from its mountain grave in the fifties and is on exhibit at the Anchorage, Alaska, airport museum. The restored *Chicago* hangs in lacquered glory in the Smithsonian's National Air & Space Museum in Washington, D.C. The restored *New Orleans* is at the Museum of Flying, Santa Monica, California.

After their Alaskan rescue, Major Frederick Martin saw to it that Sergeant Alva Harvey went to flying school. He was a major in late 1941 when he flew a B-24 bomber on a secret diplomatic mission to Moscow, and then continued around the world via the South Pacific.

Passing through Honolulu, Hawaii, Harvey chatted with his *Seattle* pilot, Martin, who then commanded the Hawaiian air defense. Two months later, after the Pearl Harbor attack, Martin was transferred along with the other Pacific area commanders. Though he did not again command abroad, Martin did so in the United States and retired as a major general.

Finally, in Florida, there is an Air Force installation involved in supporting the American initiative in space. It is called Patrick Air Force Base—a fitting memorial, for there would have been no early stick-and-canvas model for future global flight programs without the organizational and diplomatic talents of General Mason Patrick.

On Further Reading

The First World Flight—Lowell Thomas (1925). Young Mr. Thomas, at the beginning of his fame as a globetrotting journalist and popular biographer, was hired by the Air Service, after the world fliers had reached North America, to publicize their feat. This well-illustrated book is directed by the author to tell the world flight story through the alternating first-person reminiscences of the participants. This we-were-there ploy captivates the reader. Unfortunately, the volume has not been reprinted since the late 1920s, and is available only in large, long-established libraries.

Lt. Leslie Arnold kept a diary (in the library of the Smithsonian's Air and Space Museum on the Mall, Washington, D.C.) as did Lt. Jack Harding (in the Air Force Museum, Dayton, Ohio). The National Archives, Washington, D.C., has the correspondence file of the World Flight Committee; other world flight official material is in the USAF Albert F. Simpson Historical Research Center at Maxwell AFB, Alabama.

None of the world fliers wrote later at much length or of any importance about his experience. The batch of newspaper and magazine articles about the achievement at its time in 1924, and again near its anniversary in 1974, do not add many facts.

A World to Conquer—Ernest McKay (1981). The author does a good job in enlarging the background and detail of the how-and-why dimensions of the world flight in addition to retelling its story.

Round-the-World Flights—Carroll V. Glines (1982). Beginning with the U.S. World Flight of 1924, the author summarizes the following world-girdling aerial accomplishments down to 1982: dirigibles, solo flights, flying boats, bombers, airliners, spacecraft, helicopters, private planes. A heavily traveled aerial pathway.

Index

Index

The author wishes to thank F. Robert van der Linden of the Air and Space Museum of the Smithsonian Institution for his careful reading of the manuscript. Thanks also to the CAE Link Corporation, John D. Wilfley, and Mary E. Lucas for providing us with reproductions of Robert Sherry's paintings and granting permission for their use in this book.

Photo credits:

CAE Link 2, 29, 37, 54, 58, 84, 92
Library of Congress: 5, 71, 72
McDonnell Douglas/Harry Gann 8, 21, 24–25, 27, 31
First World Flight 10, 34, 43, 60, 62, 70, 90, 93, 95
National Archives 13, 14, 40, 42, 65, 69, 73, 86, 87, 94
Smithsonian Institution 15, 17, 19, 61, 76, 80–81, 89

Text quotations

46, 47 from *Blood on the Moon* by Linton Wells
82 from *Safeguarding the World Flyers* by Lyman A. Cotten, USN
93, 95 from *The First World Flight* by Lowell Thomas
Direct quotations of the world flyers come from Thomas, Arnold's and Harding's
    diaries, and magazine and newspaper accounts.